There's Nothing Going on But Your Thoughts

Reconcile with Guilt, Anger, Fear and the Past

Book 2

By Helen Gordon

PUBLISHED BY
Clearly Written
www.clearly-written.com

Copyright ©2020 Helen Gordon

All rights reserved. No part of this book may be reproduced in any form or by any means, electronic or mechanical, including photocopying, recording, or by any information storage and retrieval system, without permission in writing from the author.

Visit our website at www.helengordon.com

There's Nothing Going on But Your Thoughts – Reconcile with Guilt, Anger and the Past - Book 2/ Helen Gordon.

Second Edition

ISBN: 978-0615470535
ISBN: 061547053X

This book expresses the author's views and opinions. The information contained in this book is provided without any express, statutory, or implied warranties. Neither the author, Clearly Written, nor its resellers or distributors will be held liable for any damages caused or alleged to be caused either directly or indirectly by this book.

Cover Design by Steve Moore

Table of Contents

1. Acknowledgments ... iv
2. Foreword ... v
3. Introduction ... vii
4. Procrastination ... 12
5. Who We Are ... 12
6. Self-Forgiveness ... 19
7. The Holy Instant ... 25
8. Reality ... 30
9. Belittled ... 38
10. Eternal Life ... 44
11. Humility ... 57
12. Why the Mind Obeys the Spirit ... 62
13. Mirrors of Judgment ... 71
14. Sympathy Victimizes ... 76
15. Was the Resurrection Necessary? ... 83
16. Wizard of Oz ... 91
17. Reclaim Your Self-Esteem ... 117
18. Sacrifice is Not Necessary ... 128
19. Avoiding the Holiday Blues ... 135
20. How Do You "Let Go"? ... 143
21. Listening to the Voice ... 150
22. Pretentious Teacher ... 160
23. Footnotes ... 165

Acknowledgments

Thank you so much:

David Kensler for getting me out of my comfort zone and started on the path of my dreams. **Barbara Kensler** for her unconditional love and encouragement to write; **Jayne Whittaker** for being the best friend through my transition to writing as a career; my **ACIM students** for urging me to compile my class lectures into a book; **Marie Thomas** for archiving years of my class lectures; **Rev. Daytra Hansel, Alayne Davis** and **Elvira Bohle** for encouragement and prayer; **Maria Sauper, Marilyn Krumrey,** and **Patti Honoré** for editorial review; **Debra Karr** for her inspiration and publishing guidance; **Sean Kelly** for the perfect place to compile this book; and **Les Brown** for believing in my books. I thank **God** for them all.

Foreword
By Les Brown

Most of us have encountered change overnight. At a time when we're shifting from a domestic economy to a global economy, when foreclosures have skyrocketed, and many people are feeling powerless and hopeless, there is a voice of inspiration emerging to the forefront.

In *There's Nothing Going on But Your Thoughts*, author Helen Gordon helps you to reconnect with your personal power. Her practical methods will usher you from vision to completion.

Helen urges you to reflect on your life and determine exactly what needs to be reconciled from the inside out. You will embark on a journey that empowers you to come to grips with your past, celebrate your present, and breakthrough to your future.

Undoubtedly, *There's Nothing Going on But Your Thoughts* will propel you to move forward and free you to "get unstuck." Helen Gordon takes you on an inward voyage of self-discovery by unlocking hidden truths that lead to the manifestation of the greatness within. Get ready to conquer more than you could ever imagine.

Your past is waiting patiently for your success to begin in you. Helen Gordon gives you the tools to face your history and create a greater reality.

Les Brown
Speaker/Speech Coach/Trainer

Introduction

Have you made some choices in life you wish you could undo? Has your self-esteem plummeted? Perhaps your dreams or goals seem to be beyond your reach regardless of the effort or sacrifice you have made to make it happen. Your mental emotions are exhausted. There is not enough energy in your body to try just one more thing.

Book 2 of *There's Nothing Going on But Your Thoughts* strengthens your commitment live empowered every day. Learn how to release your tiring emotional attachment to past events; re-build your self-esteem; and inspire the creativity within you to succeed in living your dreams and purposeful life.

You have the power to do it. Nothing is beyond your reach. Nothing is impossible.

To benefit fully from this book, let go of all current beliefs, opinions, and definitions regardless of credentials, experiences, facts, or past studies. Gently put them aside somewhere while doing the exercises provided at the end of each chapter.

Introduction

Curiosity, an inner urge, and a little willingness have attracted you to this book to accept more love and its rewards. Expect this willingness to change at times. Proceed at your own pace and in private as you choose.

Resistance and anger may come and go; however, things, people, and situations show up to support you through this process. Not to worry. Let them.

At times, there may be temptation to "go back to old ways" simply because old ways are familiar and comfortable. New things can be uncomfortable at first but it is well worth the wonderful healing as you move through the process.

Ignore the urgencies of your inner critic (ego) while progressing through each chapter. The ego did not take only a few chapters (years) of your life to teach you the way you are living it. Most likely, decades of learned behavior probably will not be unlearned overnight. However, one day you will realize that you finally get it, live it, and love it. You become your own best friend and biggest fan.

Introduction

These proven exercises guide you in releasing conflict, guilt, anger and the past, and help renew your self-esteem, self-worth and commitment to your dream life.

Some exercises may seem unnecessary or feel awkward as you release the old that has not served you in meeting the goals of inner peace, health, love and prosperity that you desire. Additionally, you find that you can let go of inherited behavior, guilt, or anger and no longer have to sustain it. Change happens.

Terminology

Although Christian terminology is found in this book, it is different from its traditional usage:

- **God** has no gender. This book references God using a masculine gender for literary purposes.
- **Sin** is merely an error or misinterpretation. It can be corrected.
- **Atonement** is acceptance the error has been corrected.
- The **Holy Spirit** is your inner Voice, divine Guide, holy Spirit, and spiritual Being, that part of you which is always in communication with God. It is who you truly are, the voice for God.
- **Forgiveness** is not a pardon, but a correction in perception and the freedom to move on.
- **Ego** is the loud inner critic. Wrong-thinking. Offers unfavorable choices.
- **Illusions** refer to human being experiences.
- **Self**, in upper case, refers to your true Being that guides you rightly and is always in connection and agreement with God. It is not physical.
- **self**, in lowercase, refers to the human personality that is governed by the ego. It is physical.
- Voice is your inner guide for right choices, your holy Spirit.
- **ACIM**: A Course in Miracles.

Terminology

Gender Usage

This book utilizes masculine pronouns, traditionally the preferred usage in English literature, as representing no gender in particular. It may be helpful to mentally substitute those masculine pronouns with words like, *child, daughter, sister, her or she.*

1

Procrastination

> *"There are a few reasons we procrastinate: simple lack of interest, fear of failure, and fear of success."* – Helen Gordon

Procrastination, fear, and excuses are defense mechanisms the ego offers as a security blanket. However, procrastination is an insecurity blanket giving a false sense of control and a false sense of security.

The ego will often disguise its support as justified procrastination, giving us reasons to value its decisions for us. There are a few reasons to procrastinate: simple lack of interest, fear of failure, and fear of success. To complicate things, the lack of interest may be a distraction to support fear in accomplishing a goal.

Never be fooled again by the persistence of the procrastinating ego. It will create excuses in the form of obstacles of all sorts, distractions, lack and illness. It can appear in sheep's clothing to rekindle fear in us when stepping out to be fully who we are.

From a human perspective, all distractions can be justified by the fact of their physical existence in our lives. With this proof, delay (procrastination) is justified and the distractions made real.

Procrastination in tackling domestic chores and every day tasks are probably power struggles or rebellion of sorts. Rebellion is a power struggle in a different form. No one is going to tell us how, when or where to do anything! We'll do it when we have the time (when we darn well please!). It could be a deep seeded parental rebellion from childhood or an authoritative rebellion, which *feels* like parental control.

Just as we rebelled parents often accused of trying to control our lives, we sometimes rebel against God, the Father, as well. We avoid the commitment required to fulfill our purpose because of the seeming loss of control. What rebellion disguises here is the fear of losing control more than a fear of commitment. We want to commit but with our own rules, under our own control. And, the ego urges we will lose control through this commitment. We believe that if we lose control we lose ourselves.

This is absurd. The fact is we gain control through commitment to our purpose, as God has willed. God is all power and this power is within us. As commitment to our purpose heightens, that power is expressed through us more. Reaching a goal becomes easier to achieve because God's power guides us. Sometimes we even fear this power.

Fear is the paralysis of progress and the greatest obstacle to achieving our goals. Our goal may be a business, a friendship, or an intimate relationship. Regardless of the type of relationship, the same fears are applied to being successful in achieving them.

Also, fear paralyzes our thinking, causing us to become prisoners of our emotions or decisions. Do not avoid or deny the fear but look it square in the face to see its uselessness during the pursuit of success.

As we move forward, we are actually *allowing* our purpose to be fully expressed through us in this human experience.

We are spiritual beings having human experiences where our spiritual being gives the power to our purpose while our human being applies it in this world. Our ability to apply it is far greater than any claimed imperfection or circumstance since God is the source of all things. It is with His will that we apply ourselves to our purpose. His will cannot fail.

Neither God's plan nor our role in it was created for failure. God gave us each a gift and a goal, with the ability to succeed; otherwise, what would be the point? We must do our absolute best with no expectation of reward of any kind because **we will be rewarded automatically,** for such is the divine law.

Fear of success can also be invoked by the fear of losing love, being rejected by peers, or being rejected by loved ones. The arrogant ego will say things like, "They will think we are better than they are. We will rise above their material or intellectual levels."

Further, we think that we will no longer be able to *relate* to them on the same level or share the same values or interests. The ego says that if we prosper too much, then we will have to take care of *them*. We do not want to be responsible for them.

Humility. How cunning the ego can be (even through others' egos). Give it no power. We can remain humble in fulfilling our purpose!

Careful not to allow the ego to be a distraction by disguising itself in false humility. It may sound like: "I am so honored to..." "Look at what I have done." This will attract those who support our false humility; who stroke our ego; who validate our significance in God's will. Remember, it is the Holy Spirit who does the work. Each of us is simply the conduit for the expression of God's will on earth.

Thoughts and experiences have discouraged us from pursuing a goal, and the ego uses them as facts for why we should give up on our goal. Our goal supports our divine purpose, which creates the inner drive to reach it. The ego gathers a myriad of external influences to justify any size failure in hopes to win back our innocence. Disappointments come when the goal is unmet for we feel we have failed ourselves, our purpose.

We think we have been dealing with people and circumstances but we have been really dealing with self-disappointment. Blaming others or things merely cloud the path to our goal. The less we succumb to procrastination, the clearer we will be able to see that path. With clarity, things along that path will have different meaning and purpose.

As our perception changes, the people and circumstances in our lives will also change. Each new event will be perceived more positively than before as well as correctly. When our perceptions are of peace, our response will be at peace.

Many perceptions are based upon fear. Perceptions are what determine our reactions, so we sometimes choose incorrectly according to those perceptions by attacking. Whether it is a material thing, a person, or an egotistical loss, it is perceived as a justified attack. It is from that thinking that we make our choices.

For example, when our mate ignores us, we may become angry. We define it as rude, insensitive, unloving, and uncalled for, after all we have done! This is our interpretation of their behavior so we invite anger to stand between us where only one of us understands why it is there. Rage from the ego's perception blocks all rational thought, which blocks the clarity that communication offers.

Anger is a form of fear in this case where we fear that we will or have lost love from this person. There is a threat of separation from someone or something we feel belongs to us.

What we will learn is that we own nothing. We merely have created an illusion of ownership, which is actually a temporary condition where we have the experience of exclusivity in a special relationship.

Then there is the fear of failure. There are many commitments where procrastination is hoped to either prolong the union or strengthen it through a sense of ownership. This remains a subtle attempt to control the partner. As we can see, it indirectly attempts to control the fear while denying it.

"It didn't work...again." Procrastination should have made the whole thing disappear but avoidance failed to discard the inevitable. Self-blame dominates. "What did I do? How can I fix things?" We cannot fix anything since the situation is not incorrect. Only our perception of the seeming failure is incorrect.

With corrected perception, we will learn that everything is on purpose for a purpose. We need only to look and see how we can grow from it, bless it, and allow it to unfold divinely.

Sometimes unworthiness may creep in too, only to further drive procrastination. "I am not as good as..." is merely the ego trying to discredit God. Being one, God does not compare Itself to Itself. God did not make a mistake when He chose us for our purpose! We may fear that we do not have the "right" credentials, necessary skill level, enough money, enough time, or too old, somehow we fall short. We need not qualify by human standards for what God would have us do.

We must not tell ourselves that we must *wait until*. We are equipped now with everything we need to succeed. What we have created cannot interfere. Regardless of the appearance, we did not create our lives to be in opposition with the Will. Life was created to purposely interact in it.

We were awesomely created for our purpose. All we need was perfectly included within us and as us at conception. We were born with greatness. Our success has merely been in incubation. As a flower bud, when it is ready, it will bloom beautifully in all of its magnificence with a little of our care.

God will see to it that the color is distributed throughout each petal, that each petal fans as it should, and that the branches will grow outward and bear leaves. And when it maximizes its growth, it will pollinate to multiply itself. We need only cultivate it. Irrigate each gift with Faith and prune it with Love. This is acknowledging that all things are possible through God.

God established our worth and perfectly matched it with a purpose. We are significant here on earth because God has chosen us for our individual roles. We were chosen because we are perfect for the part. God would not have it any other way. Change nothing but willingness by increasing it.

"When the soul discerns that My Father and I are One, the door to the kingdom of heaven within will

be opened. To be with God is to be in heaven, and this is a privilege that any soul may enjoy now while yet in personal form." [1]

"To simply hope for health and freedom is to remain in our present condition however adverse that condition may be. But when we have faith in that power that can give us health and freedom, we enter into the very life of that power, and are healed at once. Faith moves on and enters directly into the very condition that is desired; it never ceases to press on until it is in the presence of that which is wanted, and therefore we can never fail.

Hope stands on the outside; faith walks in; hope waits to be guided; faith trusts its own light and proceeds; hope waits for the right opportunity; faith creates its own opportunity; hope waits to see the solid rock appearing from out the seeming void; faith goes out upon the seeming void and finds the solid rock; hope stands upon the earth eagerly looking towards the heavens; faith mounts upon the wings of the spirit and ascends to the highest heavens." [2]

Chapter 1- Exercise:

1. Write down your entire "To Do" list regardless how old some of the items may be. At the top, list five things that are older than five years.
2. Identify two things from your "To Do" list that are one month old or less.
3. Prioritize your "To Do" list, and then read it aloud.
4. Identify which ones would bring you the greatest joy.
5. Now, prioritize the list according to what would bring the most joy.
6. Today, start allowing at least 10 minutes a day (including holidays), only on the first item on your list, for 30 days.
7. Do the same for next item on the list for the next 30 days.
8. Repeat step 3 through 7.
9. Go back to the item you enjoyed the most and continue with it until it is complete. If you find there is a tie, choose the one closest to the top of the list.

2

Who We Are

"Man is always the master, even in his weakest and most abandoned state; but in his weakness and degradation he is the foolish master who misgoverns his household." - James Allen

An idea can be shared in its entirety; however, we each still have the idea fully and the next person also has it fully but it is ever depleted. As we share the idea, it is strengthened within us. The idea is strengthened among us too, which is why *we* can make a difference as individuals.

Two or more joined together reinforce the power of the oneness between us. The remembrance of our oneness is an acknowledgment of who we are, omniscient powerful beings.

We are encouraged to *be* who we are, not just *feel* or *see* who we are. Once we can *be*, it is impossible for ourselves or others not to feel and see our true Selves. As for Truth, joy, holiness, peace, and knowing, we need to just allow these elements to express through us. *Allow.* There is no need to *try,* and acceptance is key, for the rest of the good automatically follows law.

For example, when in the darkest room, if the light is turned on, the darkness must disappear immediately. There is no debate between darkness and light. Darkness must instantly obey the universal law of light. We need not *try* to make the darkness leave the room. Darkness is powerless and must succumb to the law of the presence of light.

As in any case, when the proper element is applied (in this case the light), the desire will just happen according to universal law. Mere application of this simple principle will bring about the desired result. We will not need to apply force for the darkness to go away. It is that simple. It is that effortless.

James Allen said, "*Man is always the master, even in his weakest and most abandoned state; but in his weakness and degradation he is the foolish master who misgoverns his household."*

Our household is our mind. Examine the mind to find the precious diamonds and gold of Truth within it. Within us lies a wealth of knowledge and power where real riches lay waiting claim through conscious awareness. During our self-examination, we must be patient in our search for who we are and conduct a thorough investigation of our thoughts and beliefs. As we do, we will find answers without going anywhere but right where we are in this moment.

The gift is when we remember that we were truly created powerful, having all, knowing all, and lacking in nothing. We are not fragmented beings; we are whole, complete, and united with God. The little self we have created struggles to create physical elements to *prove* its genuineness and separation from God. These elements are physical form experienced by our human being, affecting one or more of our five senses: taste, touch, smell, hearing, and sight. It can never affect the most powerful one, the sixth sense of intuition, where Truth cannot be forgotten since it is directly connected to who we truly are.

Each of the first five senses, singularly or collectively, often weakens our faith in the sixth sense, which requires no proof of its reality. Reactions of our five senses to circumstances and incidences take on such reality for us that we accept such control. We succumb to this control; hence, we respond with strong judgment, fear, and denial. As a result, we choose to accept the offerings of the ego, those things that are unreal, i.e., illusions.

The little self feels guilty for having accepted these illusions as true for reality never leaves its thoughts. Illusions do not define us, but affect our true awareness; suppress our true Self; petrify our power; and render us unintelligible.

Our sixth sense is still there, gently nudging us and feeding us Truth. This is our unexplainable restlessness, our drive to remember who we are. It is just a recognition, not something we have to become.

Take for example, a woman named Lillian. If we call her Lillian, Lilly, Mom, Sister, Aunt Lil, Ma'am, honey, boss, director or Reverend, none of these labels change who she is. They are just identity tags for her earthly relationships and for communication. They are labels of the world for role identification and nothing more.

Also, Lillian may be called some things that are not favorable such as: difficult, airhead, moron, mean or scattered. Still they are merely words of perception that do not change the Truth about her. Labels, assigned roles, anyone's perception of her, nor any other illusion can ever change Lillian's true identity as a powerful extension of God.

Lillian's true Self has never forgotten Its union with God; does not respond to the illusions; knows the questions and the answers; does not acknowledge the ego; and remains at peace at all times. Her Self communicates directly with the Holy Spirit because they still speak the same language.

God is here. He just cannot see our illusions. So He sent the Holy Spirit to communicate with us beyond our created human language. There is no communication between the ego and Spirit because they do not speak the same language, and there is no translation. Uncompromised communication can only be made in the same language. Our sixth sense assists us in that translation.

The sixth sense, our inner Voice, also assists us in remembering that our holy Spirit is eternal. It can never be destroyed or harmed because it is always in the embrace and protection of the love of God.

Fortunately, God does not use other's opinions about us to determine whether to love us or bless us. Our own images of ourselves are not used as criteria either. God allows us to express, disguise and entertain ourselves immensely to the extent that we forget who we are. Eventually we consciously reconnect with who we are, angels on earth pretending to be who we are not. Earth is the angels' theatre where we give Oscar award winning performances.

Applaud yourself for your convincing creativity.

Chapter 2 – Exercise:

Write down:

1. Write down something in your life that you have ever accomplished or overcame that amazed even you.
2. What did you do to make it happen?
3. What was your state of mind at that moment?
4. That same being is right where you are. What do you want to do next?

3

Self-Forgiveness

"God's forgiveness is instantaneous. Those things that are brought to God are remembered no more." – Helen Gordon

Something we have done or caused haunts our minds. It seems to be a life sentencing. Repeatedly, people in our lives viciously rekindle the incident to manipulate us through its guilt. Even our children learn to use the incident against us when it is beneficial to them. No matter how much we have tried to atone for it, it just seems to lurk in our lives like a nightmare, silently screaming for freedom.

This scream becomes louder, stronger, and more frequent as we try harder to *fix* it. Insanity continuously tantalizes our thoughts; cognitive degradation seems inevitable. To endure this seeming mental demise and torture, we choose drugs, sex, alcohol, food, or shopping in hope that one or all of these things will mute the scream and restore our sanity.

Those we feel were involved in the error are blamed for our nightmare. Through blame, we grant value to the incident, justify our point of view, and excuse our past behavior. Their claimed involvement is used to justify our choices, to substantiate our claims of being someone's victim, and to support our innocence.

Being a victim has elements we hold valuable that justify the type of relationship we choose to have and how we communicate in that relationship. Perceived victimization in the relationship becomes a way in which we seek to relinquish our responsibility for our miserable world and its guilt.

Victimization is used to justify not loving a person, for treating them a certain way, or for banning them from parts or all of our lives. Sometimes it is also used to prove why we are a better parent, mate, or person than someone else.

Perhaps we subconsciously seek punishment for our own participation in the incident. Whatever the form, it is vengeance on ourselves, and functionless in our journey, spiritual growth or self-esteem.

Insatiable vengeance feeds our mourning self-esteem. Vengeance merely preserves the past to abuse our minds where all control lies, weakening it until it succumbs to a deep depression. There is absolutely nothing we have ever done to deserve this depression. We must not let the ego convince us otherwise.

In time, we will tire of this self-imposed hatred that strengthens belief that we are unworthy of God's Love. Although it is impossible to be without this Love, it is possible to totally deny it in any form offered such that we no longer recognize it or feel worthy of it. The reprieve is that our worthiness for God's love is never diminished by these ridiculous thoughts.

Nothing can diminish this love. No one can diminish this love. There are no exceptions because God is fully capable of making decisions on His own and does so. Fortunately, God does not follow anyone's recommendations. Love for us is always maximal, everlasting, unconditional and not influenced by the world.

Self-Forgiveness

God declared us worthy of all He has created. Nothing can change His creation. He sees only our innocence and invites us to join His vision. In this joining, is self-forgiveness. Self-forgiveness is full acceptance of God's grace and love. It is through this acceptance we are free of past errors forever.

Welcome the Atonement. Welcome it by offering all errors to the Holy Spirit Who restores our innocence to us. Hold back absolutely nothing. Take this opportunity to clean up life's debris. Offer it in faith without judgment, regardless of the error or its intent.

The purpose of the Holy Spirit, the Comforter, is to accept the Atonement for us. It desires to fulfill this purpose; therefore, completely empty this storehouse of guilt and loveless thoughts to make room for the peace we seek.

At first, it may be difficult to let go of these things and leave them in the hands of the Holy Spirit, because we do not believe how much God truly loves us. However, through this Love, all that is brought forth is forgiven.

Self-Forgiveness

God has promised complete forgiveness simply for the asking. This promise has no expiration and readily awaits us. There is no court in which to plead for forgiveness nor is there a need to await a verdict. God's forgiveness is instantaneous for the asking. Those things that are brought to Him are remembered no more.

Chapter 3 - Exercise:

1. List one or two things you have not shaken, where you are not able to let go of the guilt.

2. Observe how your body (throat, eyes, stomach, and forehead) reacts when you think about these things identified in step 1.

4

The Holy Instant

"God is a circle whose center is everywhere, and its circumference nowhere." - Empedocles

There is a moment when you are totally engulfed in Love from some act of kindness; sometimes it brings you to tears. That is a form of a holy instant, a divine moment.

Have you experienced at least once, a crisis in which you bonded closer with someone as a result? A crisis where the least expected person showed up to support you; a crisis where your eyes were opened to the truth of an unhealthy relationship, situation, or job; or a crisis where you came to realize that you cannot do it all alone and did not have to?

The moment the bonding occurred we learned how much we cared for that person and how stabilizing they were in our lives. Each one of us answered the Call. We were matched on purpose for a purpose. God sent.

At times, we are surprised by the compassion of an unexpected person and grateful for this new expression of Love in our lives. This person touched a part of us that we were unaware of or had guarded.

As our vision was cleared, our guard was exposed for what it was and ceased to confuse fear with truth. We saw inside the magic hat and up the sleeve. Denial was no longer available. The wall dissipated to show that life could be better and happier.

We admitted that we were not a super person, and that it is okay and quite comforting to have help. In fact, it was a relief. It felt good. We could breathe!

Each of these moments of awakening is a holy instant. There is a deep and pure love experienced at that moment. That Love is God. Our Spirit acknowledged the presence of that Love through a deep heartfelt sigh and/or often tears of joy. In that instant, the Love was all there was. And for that instant, the crisis did not exist. Nothing else mattered. Life was going to be okay. All our judgments were brought to Light.

God shows up in many forms expressing His Love. His love is always here. There is never any separation from God. "I am with you always," He says.

Sometimes such a holy instant is followed up with guilt. Our Spirit welcomed this Truth but our ego felt attacked and so created guilt as an attempt to purge this Truth from our mind. Truth cannot be purged but may have that illusion when hidden beneath stacks of guilt created by the ego. In Truth, we are fully loved for longer than that holy instant.

This is the lesson. This is the message of God. For in God's eyes, we are worth it! If it were not so, we would not have had that opportunity to experience the holy instant.

We are created to teach; and in our teaching, we are guaranteed to learn as well. Questions will be many; however, there is no doubt that we will be answered because we have come seeking Truth. God cannot fail us.

Everyone in our lives is our teacher and everything in our lives supports the opportunity to apply that new knowledge and accept more love in our lives. As we do, holy instances happen frequently, eventually becoming a way of life.

Chapter 4 Exercise:

1. Write down a crisis in which you bonded closer with someone as a result.
2. What were you able to relinquish as a result?
3. How did your perception change?
4. What other positive things did you experience from the crisis?

Reality

"Forgetfulness does not destroy reality or knowledge; it merely suppresses it as an illusion we fear." – Helen Gordon

What makes for chaos and uncertainty are the number of interpretations of reality we use which have been actually learned through a social, cultural, or religious source. We fear to go against what we have been taught to avoid hell and worse yet, guilt. However, guilt creates our hell right here on earth.

Since there is often an unknown factor in our learned interpretation, fear is strengthened. We fear that which we have not personally experienced and those things we do not understand. We fear the unknown. Yet, A Course In Miracles teaches us that we must obviously fear nothing for there is no unknown. Our Internal Teacher has access to all we want to know.

Knowledge is limitless. It is very powerful; therefore, it may be power we fear since all power is of God.

Commonly, God is associated with judgment. Judgment is not from knowledge and not from God. It is merely a collection of perceived ideas and interpretations used to arrive at a conclusion we think is valid for the person, thing, or situation at hand. Judgment supports what the ego has deemed is our reality and truth.

Once our perception is of true reality, we can begin to recognize our knowledge. Perception is changeable while reality never changes. As we seek truth, knowledge returns, that is, we begin to remember what we have always known. We refer to it as enlightenment.

Since the ego wants credit for this enlightenment, it attaches a measurement to it. It assigns "levels" of enlightenment, which is really how much we choose to remember, acknowledge, and express who we are. With this seemingly innocent ranking, it creates a separation among us, creates its own justifiable adoration of certain "enlightened ones" and strips other's self-esteem and self-worth accordingly. As a result, spiritual amnesia consumes minds.

We are and will always be omniscient. We mentally retrieve from denied thoughts what is already accessible. Access to the one Mind, the library of the Universe, is unlimited.

While yearning for the conscious renewal of this omniscient power, we frantically attempt to obliterate our efforts with creative illusions, hanging on to those we value and approve. We easily approve of the illusions that say we cannot access certain knowledge. Fortunately, our approval can never make these illusions real.

Let go of these illusions lest praise and power be given to the ego. Regardless of the size, significance, or seeming harmlessness, let them all go. Illusions are illusions. These illusions are used to validate our denial as meaningful, yet we cannot give meaning to meaningless things.

Reality

The strongest reason for avoiding reality is that once we accept the power within us, we know we must accept full responsibility for the goings on in our lives as well. No longer is there anyone or anything we can assign blame. We become fully responsible for our perceptions, reactions, and outcomes. We face reality for the first time. Once we have fully embraced this knowledge, we go beyond perception to changeless reality.

Another tool used for denial and avoidance of reality is forgetfulness. Forgetfulness does not destroy reality or knowledge; it merely suppresses it as an illusion we fear. Fear is then used as justification to avoid Truth. Forgetting is a false escape from the thing we think is harmful to us.

Relinquish the fear of reality to welcome peace and understanding. It is the fantasy we created that should be feared. There is no need for interpretation of reality nor can we create it. It just is. Often there is a seeming change of reality through fantasy. However, that change can only occur in our minds.

Take a look at the reality we have created for ourselves. Is it ideal for a child of God? Does love dominate it? Is it a safe place to rest our heads?

We have creative minds that do not lose creative abilities for experiencing the world it created. Creating is its nature. Alternatives, different paths, and altered outcomes continue to be created one fantasy after another.

A Course In Miracles says, *"The test of everything on earth is simply this; 'What is it for?' The answer makes it what it is for you. It has no meaning of itself, yet you can give reality to it according to the purpose that you serve."* [3]

Eventually the fantasy expires, (it can only last so long, being temporary) because the mind can no longer nurture it, so its creator becomes disappointed, depressed, and sometimes enraged. By-products of the created experiences such as situations, conditions, and people are declared the reason things did not work out. This false reality (fantasy) revealed itself as unreal, and then disappeared. The illusions are the nightmares, bad luck, and crisis in our lives; however, we are freed from these illusions through true reality.

Reality is the journey within to experience what God created. The journey is anticipated to be difficult, but it is simple. The simplicity of the journey will be often perceived as difficult when it presents ideas very different from what has been learned from sources outside of us. Look beyond the "different" to shine continuous light on this path to remain clear and in sight of Truth. With us is always a spark of the Light that removes the darkness.

"It is not arrogant to be as He created you or to make use of what He gave to answer all His Son's mistakes and set him free. But it is arrogant to lay aside the power that He gave, and choose a little senseless wish instead of what He wills.

The gift of God to you is limitless. There is no circumstance it cannot answer, and no problem which is not resolved within its gracious light." [4]

We cannot create our true Selves, thank God for that. God already did that for us. But, often we do look more to the shadow and say it is us. That shadow takes on monstrous shapes, meanings, and intentions. We become so caught up in the further creativity of illusions that we believe they are real, get distracted, and fear the light.

Light casts out darkness without effort when it is introduced in a room because that is the law of light. This law intimidates the ego because it fears exposure of its lies and weakness.

Allow the light to illumine your powerful capabilities. Move toward the light to dim the destructive fear the ego has offered. As we do, our blinded vision is made clear again; we see clearly the inviting spiritual path that leads to divine destinations of our lives.

There is only one Truth and it does not change by season, by person, by circumstance, by agenda, or for any reason.

Chapter 5 - Exercise:

1. If you have used the expression, *what's true for me...* or *my truth is...* look to see if any aspect of it has changed over time. The ego will send you to the ones of significant change, but any change is significant for the lesson you are learning right now.

2. Identify incidences where reality changed for you.

6

Belittled

> "The real Self cannot be attacked, belittled, or de-valued in any way by the ego's words, thoughts, or actions. It can only remain magnificent, powerful, and valuable."
> – Helen Gordon

Be still and listen. When giving, be still and listen. In that still moment, the ego is silenced for it cannot mute the Voice of Truth as it speaks to us. Both cannot speak at the same time; therefore, the ego must wait until granted permission to be heard. We control that waiting period. Let the Self control all thoughts as the ego waits for an invitation to be heard. During this moment, the ego is rendered powerless to the divine Self.

The Self cannot be attacked, belittled, or de-valued in any way by the ego's words, thoughts, or actions. It can only remain magnificent, powerful, and valuable. The real Self wants to fulfill the Will of God, fears nothing of this world and remains anchored in Its oneness with God. This is who we truly are at any given instant of earthly time.

This Self is our Spirit, housed by our physical bodies. It never forgets who It is or Its relationship with God. The Self is real and knows only true reality created by God. An attempt to strip away any bit of reality will only cause it to *seem* non-existent in our own lives. The ego's reality would then gain influence. There is nothing to gain from such influence since ego reality is valueless.

The ego will try to win us over by offering appealing forms, which appear to define its value or to offer immediate gratification. Choose again. Choose only those things of value. It is simple to do. However, the ego will make it appear difficult because it senses rejection. If we reject what the ego offers, it will throw guilt as an obstacle before us at each step on the path to Truth.

It will bombard us so heavily with guilt that we tire of dodging, ducking, and jumping through hoops to escape this guilt we really never had. Whenever wearied of some pressing issue, relax and breathe deeply then say, "I am valuable. God values me. I am precious in His eyes."

As we embody this Truth more each day, the ego may be unconsciously granted a guest pass sometimes in our lives in time of uncertainty, but it will never have control again. We will watch its tricks and games as an audience being entertained because we no longer choose to participate in what is valueless.

During holidays and family gatherings, perhaps, we will engage in joking around. Some joking includes put-downs meant as friendly gestures. Those put downs will also help us identify areas of fear and what to release to the Holy Spirit if we observe our reactions Our participation diminishes with time as we value them less and less.

When we look at those put-downs, we will find that most of them we do not believe ourselves, never did, but they have been taught to us. We picked them up from somewhere else, who knows when.

Sometimes the put-downs are expressed to "fit in" the conversation at hand, the camaraderie, or perhaps to project guilt or attention onto someone else. If we can point out someone else's faults in jest, the ego thinks it distracts attention from our own faults or justifies them.

Put-downs of ourselves can often be harsher than ones from others. We are more forgiving of other's shortcomings than our own. It is not uncommon for put-downs to be echoes of our parents, siblings, teachers, or other voices from the past. We no longer need to accept their ego beliefs about us. This corpse of put-downs negatively ignites our emotions.

Most often we are reacting to conditions of the past, not the issue at present or the person at present. This is also why forgiveness is necessary for often the person is not really attacking us, they are responding to their past. These put-downs of the past, which had so much impact in the past, are *buttons* today. When they get pushed (subconsciously remembered), reaction is as if the issue was happening in the present.

We can choose again to finally erase those things of the past that do not serve us today. This book will push many buttons as well as identify new ones, but do not get discouraged. The buttons come forth to be healed and erased.

Most buttons are in response to "what will people think." Allow time to look within for the answers and to identify where the ego has dug up the past and dumped it into the present, like buried toxic waste.

We must forgive ourselves. God has forgiven us; all we need to do is accept this to be true. Also, forgive others so that the guilt of the matter does not live on with us and does not push buttons in our relationships and in situations that remind us of it.

Divine memory is returning and we choose to remember even more while listening in the silence. Some of the exercises we will find comforting. It is okay to use them when needed in daily situations. I encourage it. This is called applying the principles presented in this text. It is the best way to release the ego beliefs disrupting our lives.

Other exercises we will resist for they threaten to open a door that we would prefer to remain closed. Let it open so the frightened little self can escape its prison. Freedom is its cherished desire, valuable beyond desire.

Chapter 6 - Exercise:

Write down:

1. If you participate in joking around using put-downs, what do you say?
2. Is it something you would say about yourself?
3. Why or why not?
4. What put-downs do you say about yourself in private?
5. Is it true?
6. Is it an opinion you have accepted?
7. Is it new or old?
8. Where did it come from?
9. How would you correct that put-down statement?
10. Replace it with a positive statement whether you believe it or not or whether you feel comfortable with it or not.
11. Whose put-downs annoy you?
12. Why?
13. What is your relationship with that person?
14. What would you like to say to that person (whether he/she is alive or not)?

7

Eternal Life

"Consider a burning candle: its life is also its death; death and life constantly interact. Just as one cannot experience true joy without having suffered great pain, so life is impossible without death, for they are a single process. Death is life in another form."
- Philip Kapleau

No one gets out of life dead. Death does not cease life. We are eternal beings. We never die. Life **is** eternal.

Life is experienced in different forms of the human body for our spiritual being, through us, through loved ones who are here, and through those who have ascended. The body returns to dust after a time but we live on.

What lives on is our spiritual Being, that is, who we really are, always have been, and always will be. Our spiritual Being existed (had life) before our human body formed and will live forever after that body is gone.

A Spirit does not know or experience death, yet we grieve as if it does. Death cannot be ignored, but it can be perceived differently. The ego's perception of death is one of guilt and loss. It usually creates a need for self-punishment, a strong sense of guilt, and a great deal of pain for both the dying and the survivor. However, death is not a punishment for any reason nor is anyone guilty of the seeming loss. No one has to grieve or repent for a lifetime.

A heart may have pain hidden even from itself. One deeply hidden pain is often grief for the loss of another human being. Grief can be hidden so deep that reactions to many things that seem non-related are really subconscious remembrance of a particular loss.

For example, tragic news reports and movies of tragedy, which involve death, can trigger an emotional experience of a past loss. Remembrance of that personal loss is resurrected for a moment. This subtly adds to the anxiety of the moment, a thief of the inner peace we so treasure and seek.

Enormous energy is used to avoid all things suspected to activate the recollection of that loss. Those things are shoved deeply beneath our outer expression, hidden from our conscious emotions.

Hidden grief is denial used as an emotional survival tool. The grief is too unbearable to face head on. However, its denial is useless and reveals itself in destructive and obsessive behaviors. We hope that somehow ignoring it might make it magically vanish. It will not vanish because physical death will not reverse over the years once complete. As we begin to understand death, grief's pain diminishes.

Naturally, we must have our human experience. Grieving is one of them, but through the grieving, remember that there is no separation between the deceased, God, or us. Physical bodies take a new form; however, the Spirit remains formless, unharmed, and perfectly whole as it was before inception on this earth.

There is one big lesson to learn from death: **There is no separation**! We are all extensions of God, that is, members of the **one** Mind. We are one in Spirit! And that never changes.

Fortunately, life does not begin on earth nor does it end on earth. As far as the human being is concerned, life is defined as an active breathing body. This active physical body and other's interaction with it is what is used to define life on earth as a reality while the involuntary permanent inactivity of the physical body is defined as death.

Reality does not begin at birth nor cease with death. Reality always was and always will be. We are Spiritual beings first, of eternal form, having created human experiences in a finite form we call reality. The drama, the fantasy, and the illusions were created at a level of complexity for remembering our connection with God's eternality and pure Love.

The authors take on life, death, and choices:

We are the authors of our own life's novel. This tends to be difficult to comprehend or accept given some of the dramatic experiences we have endured. So we question why we chose such tragedy and trauma in our created lives.

As a Spiritual being, we knew only reality, love, and God, having no experiences of the ego thought process yet or its outcomes. With that knowledge, we enthusiastically created a life that would not be boring. Participants, that is, other Spirit siblings, agreed to give Oscar winning performances for us to achieve an entertaining earthly experience and vice versa. Their roles in our lives support the relationship required for our specific human experience.

In spite of our novel, our spiritual Self remains pure, ever knowingly connected to other spiritual Beings. We are never separated from our spiritual siblings (referred to as angels). This is impossible.

All Spirits are children of God as well as extensions of God. An extension of God can never be separate from God. God cannot be separate from Itself. There is no need. A spiritual umbilical cord cannot be severed. Therefore, when someone dies, they are not separated from us. They have merely come to the end of their personal novel of life here on earth, which sometimes has an element of surprise. Applaud them and help celebrate their creative finale of life.

The movie star's death scene is always the last chapter. If not, what would define the end of the story, and what would define life? This last scene could be a murder, car crash, suicide, natural causes, or peaceful. Whatever the finale, grieve not how someone has written the last chapter of their novel. It is but a fantasy, an illusion, that can only be experienced as a human being. Only through the ego can this illusion be experienced as real because God has no interest in illusions or lovelessness.

Nothing about life can destroy who we truly are in any way. Illusions are harmless. Knowing we cannot be destroyed, our novels were to be so creative in molding this human expression called life and authored from a pure spiritual mind with no ego intervention. Ego is merely an invisible powerless character.

Some of us chose to support (play a role in) another Spirit's human experience. We are characters in their life's novel, which we willingly accepted as part of our human experience too. Scenes in each Spirit's novel interact. They are schools and human life is the curriculum.

What is assigned in the curriculum is found in a chapter of our novel. When we initially authored our lives, we knew it would have a happy ending, a happy ever after. All Spirits know this before Its human creation takes form. We wanted this world in order to have this human experience and we got it. Earth is our stage, our playground.

We all return to God as angels (Matthew 22:29), in a manner as we authored, to pure thought, that is, transcend the ego. The ego's existence is totally erased from all thoughts as we let go of this human body and its life as we know it. Life, as we created it, no longer has any significance but returns to what it always was, nothing.

The ego uses social definitions associated with time to convince us that this life's novel (fiction) is real. The ego uses time (age) for support and to substantiate its existence and to attempt to prove these events are real and powerful. It also uses time and age to urge us to dislike God, calling Him unfair, partial, and cruel. God did not *allow* any bad things to happen in our lives, we wrote it into the script ourselves.

People ask, "But what about the babies? They are too young to make a decision for themselves!" Spirits have no gender, no age, and all are equally omniscient. Therefore, death of a child should be no more a sad affair than that of an eighty-year-old person. Although death may have been expected, mourning is just as strong for the elder one.

How often do we hear someone say, "Well it was his time," simply because of age? Age seems to pardon death for the aged. Only the ego would assign a value to perfectly equal Spirits. An eighty-year-old person has not necessarily lived a *fuller* life than a child.

The elderly have not *earned* death, making it more socially acceptable that death has come to their bed. Age was not a factor, our authorship was. Some Spirits chose only to experience a human body (through miscarriage, abortion, crib death, etc.) and no further.

The ego refers to infant death as tragic, that the "baby had no chance" at life. The baby is an ageless Spirit, no younger or older than another adult or child (Spirit), no younger or older than we are right now. Even a "short" life can fulfill the human experience that that Spirit scripted for Itself. Length of human life is a choice not a sentence.

For a moment, I want you to become a novelist from a Spirit's perspective. Pretend you are a pure Spirit, a virgin of human experience, who can only see things from a pure perspective of Love and lack of judgment. Other Spirits are invited to help you as you request. Each Spirit is the same age and all have gathered to co-author a novel about a family, with each Spirit creating a character for Itself. Creating these characters is amusing. We have a blast creating our story (life experience).

A really way out character might be fun, but it is only pretend so we do not concern ourselves about whether it will change us, being the authors of this fictional story. We even plagiarize tragic events of others. Tragedy just makes it more interesting we think so we throw some in. (Isn't that what makes a bestseller?) Each Spirit agrees to come to this earth, play their part, have fun with it, and then return to who they are. An Oscar performance comes natural for each Spirit as they unite as family, friends, acquaintances, or colleagues.

Some of the characters die off (return home) at the beginning of the plot; some do not. The villain stays on to keep things interesting and to keep the tension going. Each Spirit in the collaboration have agreed that it will be a dramatic human experience. This is really going to be fun they think!

Did you create a character? Although we will always be eternal beings, we must create a body to house our Spirit while playing Its role in this human experience. What that body will become even shows creativity. What we create is only a role and character, not a separation from God.

Now that we know these things are all harmless, we can freely love others unconditionally since each person we encounter is just living out their fictional drama role just as we are. They can enjoy their experiences, knowing their connection with God is not affected.

We created the ego to help us in this created reality of supporting actors. Jesus knew it would be difficult to enjoy life with the constant engagement of ego thoughts. For spiritual support, the Voice accompanied us here to remember reality for us.

Jesus showed us it could be done!

Once our Spirit inhabited this self-created body, it had to be able to remember who it was. This was easy to know as a pure Spiritual being without the ego.

Although it was fun creating the lives we live, the Spirit had no idea it would be so difficult to play the role because its thoughts are foreign to "not knowing" everything. Our Spirits cannot separate from us, other Spirits, or from God. It is impossible. We are one in Spirit, all members of the one body, forever creating.

So those of us who have lost their precious ones to death, not to worry. They loved us purely before they joined us and love us as purely now. When they left, their love did not diminish but became once again 100% unconditional. No one ever leaves us because angels are what we return to being when we are in our pure Spirit form.

Yes, angels are always assisting each other. They are our spiritual siblings. The Voice remembers to summon them as we need. They arrive in a form we can most easily accept in our lives to assist us in the manner we need at that instant. As light, they illumine the path we have chosen to experience, that is, rekindle our awareness of our creative choice.

It is the approach of light, the awareness, that feels threatening. The ego fears we are about to illumine the path to joy, to experience the joy it has been trying to hide from us through its darkness. We are closer to remembering more!

In our attempt to remember, we access our divine understanding, that which is not of the ego. Awareness feels like knowing more but is only remembrance. As our memory returns, we remember how to take the pen of the Voice and begin to edit our earthly lives. After all, we are the Editor-In-Chiefs. Let's enjoy life.

Chapter 7 - Exercise:

1. Identify some moments when your role in someone's life was not perceived as pleasant.
2. Could the experience have been unpleasant without their permission?
3. Identify someone whose role has not been pleasant in your life.
4. What would you edit in your life's novel today? How would you physically change it?
5. Do you think your parents, siblings, children or friends also have this option? What restrictions do you put on them in their life's journey?

8

Humility

"Man often expresses arrogance in the name of humility." - Helen Gordon

"The hen knows when it is daybreak, but allows the rooster to make the announcement." – Ashanti Proverb

Only the ego values arrogance, which is sometimes denied in the name of humility. Under the disguise of humility, the ego will have us:

- Seek approval of others to validate our self-worth.
- Claim authority on something.
- Believe we have been granted special power, exude self-confidence, and appear under control.
- See subservience and lack in others often.
- Become socially selective.

What the ego has in fact offered is fear. Every one of these disguises is a form of fear where a plea for Love is severely distorted. The ego teaches us that if we master these things, we will be "liked" and "accepted" in spite of who we think we are.

What appears to be an inflated ego (arrogance) is actually a desperate attempt to mask and deny the insecurity hiding behind the outward arrogance, a guard against exposure of who we think we are. Who we think we are has been deemed unworthy by our own little secret judgments, hidden even from ourselves.

At great costs, we invest in being liked through cosmetic changes, academic achievements, impressive clothing, and certain life styles. Maintaining these investments becomes an obsession. The desperate goal is to receive approval in these areas, which is artificial love.

Although the small bits of artificial love are very gratifying to us, they are temporary due to the law of its ego source. Needing to experience this love again and again develops into various unhealthy relationships with food, drugs, alcohol, money, etc.

Artificial love is insatiable and turns these relationships into degrading dependencies.

All things in which arrogance seeks comfort, such as love or security, are provided in true form when we respond through sincere humility. Its rewards are real and satisfying.

Whether it is a fight for a cause, perfection of our gift, or success in our career, it is all a fulfillment of our purpose in some form. We have a holy purpose, an idea of God to be made manifest here on earth. Through humility, it will gracefully unfold to meet a blessed goal, rewarding those who join us and blessing those who receive us.

It can be a challenge to have those who join us to remain humble; therefore, we must be the example to follow.

Arrogance depends upon the ego's directives. Humility obeys only the will of God because it mutes the voice of the ego. It does not respond to self-gratification in any form nor seek to receive. Through our true humility, we only seek to serve and to be of service. As a result of this service, we receive our rewards.

As we serve, we are never excluded from the blessings of receiving any good. What is done for others is returned to us many times over. That is the law of giving. Since this is the law of giving, having our needs met are never an issue. Listen to the divine Voice within and follow it joyfully home.

Chapter 8 - Exercise:

1. Write down what you think humility means without looking in the dictionary.
2. Write down the areas where you feel you demonstrate humility.
3. Write down the areas where you do not.
4. Write down the names of five people you feel are humble or have shown humility.
5. What traits do you have in common with each of the five people in step 4?
6. Are they the same areas?
7. Write down the names of five people you feel are arrogant.
8. Identify which ones are successful in the public eye and why.
9. What are your similar traits to those in step 7 even if the similarity is weak?

9

Why the Mind Obeys the Spirit

"Nothing serves the body, yet we give it authority over the mind and Spirit."
- Helen Gordon

Do you think of yourself as a Body, Mind and Soul? With this trinity, we attempt control over people, situations and circumstances in our lives. The body is the weakest of the trinity of our human experience, yet we try to give it authority over the mind and Spirit. It is the Spirit the mind must serve and the mind which the body must serve. Nothing serves the body.

Since we experience our human being through our body, we naturally give the body utmost significance and tremendous value. Some even become obsessed with its look and mechanics. Cosmetics, surgery, and bodybuilding are some of the things used obsessively to maintain the value we have assigned our bodies.

It is quite difficult not to assign the body some human defined value when its physical appearance looks back at us in the mirror each morning, during the day, and at the close of the day. Wherever we go, there it is.

In this trinity, we are Spirit, mind, and then body. This is also the hierarchy of our power since it is the Spirit (Soul) which has complete authority over the others. To gain control over our lives, we must use the power of this hierarchy correctly every day. As we do, goals and tasks will begin to unfold easily.

Elements necessary in the success of our goals will come forth to assist us when we remember this hierarchy of power. Acknowledge and accept this position of the Spirit who remembers respects and harmonizes with the will of God. Each Spirit created its human life but not in conflict with the will of God. Therefore, those things which happen in our lives cannot harm nor change what God has purposed regardless of our change in goals, priorities, or beliefs. Our changes will affect only our personal human experience.

The spirit-created mind, the one which is allowed ego influence, often denies the mind of the Spirit, vying for sole power over the body. This denial is the ego's attempt to keep the mind unconscious so it can control us better. In this denial, the ego feasts and seems to strengthen its influence in our life's affairs.

Allow the mind to join in the consciousness of the Spirit, then watch the body become more appreciative. Although we may allow the ego to express through the mind and body, release it quickly or disease will surely attack them. When the ego is allowed to dominate the orders given to the body, the body struggles in chaotic decision and obedience.

This chaotic decision manifests as headaches, depression, hypertension, heart problems, eating disorders and many stress-related diseases. The mind receives feedback from the body, denies the disease it has given it, and then feels guilty.

In an attempt to rid itself of this guilt, it gathers medical, social and all kinds of supportive "facts" to justify its denial. Facts merely magnify the drama and intensify those things which "prove" why life has been unfair to us, our children, our families and chosen others. Begin to feed the mind healthier things that those healthy things are made manifest in life. Healthy thoughts reduce life's drama.

Drama serves only the ego. Sometimes it is disguised as martyr-like giving to the community, the children, the poor, the beaten and the downtrodden. Yet, that drama is feeding the ego through different forms, strengthening in others' minds the acceptance and joining in the ego's reality of those incidences and conditions. Instead, feed the mind only true reality. Feed true reality to others so it weakens the daily drama that seems to appear even more.

Let go of the drama.

Release the mind of all guilt. Forgive it and let the mind be healed and returned to its wholeness. How do we do this?

Ask for understanding.

Truly ask for understanding, not just for an explanation of why it seems you are being punished or being victimized. Avoid facts to support situations or circumstances claimed to be ruining your life. Before asking for this understanding, put aside any judgments about the situation, any conclusions and let go of any anxieties, resentments, obligations or grievances around it for a moment. Really clear your mind of any blockages to hear the Answer.

Ask in silence, and then most importantly, listen. During this silence, do not judge what you hear. Release any opinions about it whatsoever. You want life to love you.

Accept the Answer.

From the Answer, learn the lesson before you. You may not like the lesson, but it either is because you do not fully understand the Answer, resist the Answer, or deny it. If this should occur, take a deep breath and dismiss the session. Try acceptance again another time in the same or next day.

Pray for openness.

Pray for openness and open your ears. Try again to accept the Answer. A day or two later, is recommended. When more than two days lapse, the ego will begin to bury it deep in your cellar of resentment where it will emerge as a stress-related disease.

Let the incident go.

Talk it out just once, completely, and with someone neutral, but it need not be rehashed at every subsequent opportunity. Telling your *story* to everyone who will listen is not advisable. The alleged support builds upon the very anger you are trying to release. It is also unhealthy, causing you to re-live the emotion that came up during the incident, aggravating the body's functioning.

End the story

Rehashing your drama (*sharing* your story) merely feeds the greed of victimhood as comfort and escape. Nothing more is given to or taken from you or anyone else. You are only weakened and made to hunger for more drama to feed the insatiable ego.

Repetition of a story is usually indicative of guilt. If you can prove to others that you had nothing to do with the circumstances, you think your innocence will be restored. Then, no person or God will hold it against you.

Deep down, this goal is never satisfied. It is insatiable because you are attempting to fix something that is not broken. You are guilty of nothing and your innocence is unchanged. It was merely an error in thinking which you desire to correct. Allow the Spirit to correct your mind to heal your body.

Spirit rules the mind, which rules the body. Keep this hierarchy in the forefront of all thoughts. Remember this in all circumstances, situations and events of life. Accept the power of the Spirit and live life fully, allowing this human experience to be enjoyed. Our Spirit is our guide and our minds open to what It has to teach us.

There is no exam or requirements of any kind to pass or fail life. Nothing of our past has the power to prevent our healing but with our allowance. It is self-condemnation which blocks our healing. Our opinion of ourselves is not God's vision of us. God wants us to be happy.

Listen to what the Spirit hears from God, "I love you my child. I will forever love you." Then tell the body just that. We do not have to believe it to do it. Eventually the mind and our acceptance will catch up, thus our enlightenment will also expand, love will become more present in our lives and our spirituality will deepen .

Chapter 9 - Exercise:

With this exercise, you will become aware of how the Spirit feeds the mind and how the body responds to thought.

Do at least one of the following each day:

1. Feel the ground beneath your feet with every step. It is there to support you. Let it. The ground may be carpet, a footrest, cement, soil, grass, sand, etc. If you are unable to walk, become aware of whatever is beneath your feet or is supporting your body.

2. Feel the air against your cheeks, lips and eyes. (air from outdoors, air-conditioning, or heat)

3. Close your eyes and gently rub a rich scented hand cream into your hands, and then rest your hands on your lap or atop your desk. For a full minute, watch the back of your hands with your inner eye. Feel and see the hand cream penetrate your skin as it nourishes and strengthens each cell. Do this for a full minute at least three times today.

10

Mirrors of Judgment

"Mirrors are often not exact mirror images since it is not the desire of the ego to have our illusions obvious." – Helen Gordon

The positive is a mirror just as the negative can be a mirror. Negative is not always negative, although it may appear so at that moment. In fact, it is usually not negative, but our ego may establish it so through interpretation.

For example, a *stubborn* personality trait mirrors determination and commitment. When we see something in someone else, do not automatically judge it as negative or it is easy to deny the mirror and avoid what is really being mirrored. Our negative interpretation of the mirroring reveals who we think we are. When such terror and attack come in to play, the illusions are built. However, positive mirrors will appear!

Not all mirrors are direct mirror images. A rapist intends to manipulate, control, exert power, and influence to get something without regard to the victim's future condition. Sales persons also do this, but for monetary rewards where the victim is called client or customer. So here we have an example of a mirror but not a direct mirror image. Only the form is different. Their self-serving motives are the same.

Take a personal judgment of another person and seek that issue in one's self. What we see in someone else surely exists in our own lives; it is mirrored somewhere in our activities or thoughts. However, the form can distort it and make it invisible.

For example, our judgment of someone who appears to not have control of their eating habits is that they are overweight. Our solution to their alleged problem is that they change their eating habits and commit to a healthy diet.

Where in our lives are we not putting forth committed effort to complete a project or make a positive change? What project is in our garage or closet that is still on our "to do" list? What book still needs to be read or bought; what room still needs painting; what work area still needs to be organized? Do we need to drop some pounds too?

Take a look at life's hint this person has brought to you, and then take action regardless of the form of the needed change. The form may make it difficult to recognize; however, look at the different forms the judgment may have expressed so far.

Mirrors are often not exact mirror images since it is not the desire of the ego to have our illusions obvious. Sometimes we experience the mirrored traits in different parts of our lives, in different forms, and with different motivations. Find out where a trait is being mirrored. It may be in an area where we can use it positively. Look everywhere: attire, reading, habits, job, hobby, or domestic skills; it could be anywhere.

The ego will try to convince us that our judgment of someone is mirrored in some very seriously devastating place in our lives in order to persuade us to avoid looking at it. Avoidance causes us to become anxious and fearful. We begin to exert enormous amounts of energy trying to avoid seeing ourselves.

What we see in others is an answer to a question we have not consciously asked yet. It could also be an answer to a question we have asked repeatedly and wondered why we have not been answered.

Basically, the answer is in the judgment. Clarity is right before us. Directions on what we need to do in regards to the question are right before us. In our judgment statement, we may have even stated the answer and then the solution if we but listen. What a blessing it will be to finally look at ourselves.

Everyone we judge is here to support us in reaching a goal for our highest good, for expediting our spiritual deepening, and for doing our work. Our perfect imperfections are such a blessing. We thank everyone who we feel has any imperfection because it brings us the answer to our inquiry.

Chapter 10 - Exercise:

1. Write down a judgment you make of others that seems to repeat itself.
2. Write down another one.
3. Go deeper in your thinking and ask what is really being judged.
4. Where is that trait or activity in **your** life?
5. What is it answering?
6. What can you do about it?

11

Sympathy Victimizes

"Sympathy is a joining of the ego's belief that circumstances can change or destroy our divineness." – Helen Gordon

No one needs sympathy. Lack of sympathy may appear cruel but sympathy is only a gift of the ego. It merely strengthens the lie about the person we wish to support. Sympathy is used to validate what is reality in one's life according to the ego's interpretation.

Acceptance of the ego's interpretation is not supportive of anyone. Sympathy is a joining of the ego's belief that circumstances can change or destroy our divineness. Supporting the ego's interpretation of a situation is a form of denial and distraction from the positive opportunity at hand.

Opportunities to heal emotionally, physically, and financially stand before the person. However, do not deny the pain the person claims to feel. At that moment, it is real for them but is resolvable with Truth. The next step is unveiling the Truth about the situation. Respond to their cry for love, which appears as solicitation of sympathy. Perhaps they are saying, "Notice me, hug me, listen to me, believe me, or love me."

Meet them on that level without joining in the emotions of the circumstance. Remain focused on the source of the pain, not the pain itself. The pain is only a by-product of a deeper issue, which is fear of the deprivation of love and fear of looking at the pile of guilt constructed high from it.

With sympathy, the person submerges more into the illusion, giving in to the pain. Sympathy falsely validates or *prove*s the alleged lack, strengthening what is perceived as the world against them. Whatever happens next is usually blamed on the circumstance, which by now has gathered even more supporters from their "story" campaign.

All join in to agree that any seeming failure is due to this suffering, not what has or has not been done to make a change. The person claims no responsibility for their life's pain. Energy is then used to nurse the illusion, avoiding the source of the circumstance. Clarity of the source could actually bring healing or correction.

Too much sympathy also breeds contempt, resentment, and other forms of emotional chaos. It is extremely crippling. When a person does not sympathize on our behalf, they are seen as cold, cruel, and unloving; they become the enemy. We accuse them of not understanding our position and not being understanding of it. As a result, a relationship of conflict is created with whoever rejects our ego's solicitation for sympathy.

Anger and resentment raise their ugly heads against this alleged non-sympathetic person. Each encounter with the person now worsens the repressed issue, where their *attitude* is added to the list of things we claim is "holding us back." Certainly they are guilty of contributing to our demise or failures. Because of their seeming non-support, we claim that we are not able to move forward. Stuck. Scarred for life. Their lack of sympathy becomes somewhere else to place blame, burying the original issue even deeper.

As a result, the relationship becomes strained and a new issue is born. That relationship does not need healing, our interpretation does. "They" did not create the original issue nor can they heal it. Only we can do that.

We are entirely responsible for a change in our situation. To hold others innocent would mean taking responsibility and facing up to our created little disguises that the ego intended for denial and avoidance. The relationship strain compounds the original issue, which makes it seem even more devastating.

Guilt is projected onto the other person with thoughts such as, "If they cared... (then they would accept my ego's view), they would sympathize with me and join me in my darkness." Face the guilt within because we really know they are not these labels we have given them. Why draw them into a darkness where they cannot support us to heal.

Facing up to the deep issue is what we fear most because we think it must surely condemn us of something. This fear makes it feel impossible to be rid of the guilt surrounding it. We think we are responding to guilt when we are really responding to fear. The real issue is not as fearful as we think. In fact, bringing it to light is not harmful to our well being at all; it is helpful. It is actually our key to releasing the garbage that is weighing down our minds and robbing us of the peace and happiness we are really seeking.

As long as the ego can keep us fearful, then we will not pursue happiness or recognize it. It will continue to waltz us around the issue, ducking, dodging, and avoiding the thing we think condemns us. Anyone who attempts to lead us directly to our hidden issue without presenting a detour is attacked.

When they bring the light, their role in our lives is misinterpreted; therefore, we remain closed to their divine support. How they have chosen to respond to our needs does not meet our expectations. Someone who satisfies our expectations is welcomed. Those offering the most pity are embraced. However, this only draws people and situations to us who support our interpretation and fear.

Sympathy Victimizes

Do not hold anything against anyone who is not supporting our sympathetic thoughts. They are merely fulfilling the role we have created for them and their duty is to do it well. They are in our lives to remind us of what we think about ourselves, not to recruit victims or submit our names to God for condemnation.

What do we think about ourselves? What do we think we deserve in life? Are we trying to fulfill our requirements of what God wants from us or someone else's version of it? God has no such requirements. He wants us to have and enjoy our every desire. Changing our thoughts will draw to us what we desire.

We were not created by mistake. Since everything God creates is valuable, we are invaluable. We were created by God, created perfectly just the way we are and just the way we are not. God will continue to embrace us in unconditional love until we awaken from our own created nightmare. Wake up and see the Truth.

Chapter 11 - Exercise:

1. Write down the name of a person or group for which you had strong sympathy.
2. Write down the benefits you think you obtained from your sympathy.
3. Write down the benefits the person or group received from your sympathy.
4. What is the current state of the person or group for which you had sympathy?
5. Identify a relationship where conflict entered because sympathy or agreement with you did not happen.
6. How has that relationship developed?

Was the Resurrection Necessary?

"In spite of all the miracles, there was yet doubt and fear. What more could Jesus have done to convince us of our eternality, but to use an extreme situation such as the resurrection?" – Helen Gordon

The crucifixion was an unspoken demonstration of forgiveness and defenselessness. *"I elected, for your sake and mine, to demonstrate that the most outrageous assault, as judged by the ego, does not matter."*[5] *"The resurrection demonstrated that nothing can destroy truth,"*[6] and that the ego can be transcended. Nothing the ego has created can change the immortality God has promised us.

The crucifixion was not a form of punishment. It was intended to teach us that we could not be persecuted. *"If you react as if you are persecuted,*

Was the Resurrection Necessary?

you are teaching persecution. Teaching persecution is real merely denies your own salvation. Rather, teach your own perfect immunity, which is the truth in you, and realize that it cannot be assailed. Do not try to protect it yourself, or you are believing that it is assailable." [7] *"I am the model for rebirth, but rebirth itself is merely the dawning on your mind of what is already in it."* [8]

Through the resurrection, God offered the Atonement; Jesus accepted on our behalf. As a Spirit in flesh, he demonstrated that even in human form we could see peace in the midst of adversity.

Jesus was an example, not an exception, having no greater power or abilities than us. He claims only equality with us. In John 14:12 in the New Testament of the Bible regarding miracles, he says, *"…anyone who has faith in me will do what I have been doing. He will do even greater things than these, because I am going to the Father."* [9] Jesus does not doubt our abilities. What better confirmation of our abilities than this Biblical passage?

Was the Resurrection Necessary?

Also, Jesus apparently had no particularly unique physical characteristics that distinguished Him from the other disciples. If so, Judas would not have had to kiss him to identify him among the disciples or anyone else. They (enemies) knew him not from any other, according to the Bible. Apparently, Jesus saw no value or real necessity to dress or groom differently than His disciples. Again, he was displaying equality with the disciples.

For many years, Jesus observed, studied, and then taught, demonstrating that our human experiences are harmless. These demonstrations were through His performance of many miracles through hands-on healings or implicit declarations.

Miracles addressed chronic illness, terminal illness, handicaps, and even death. The miracles were meant to take away fear associated with afflictions, circumstances or conditions of any kind. Jesus demonstrated how time, distance, medical facts, diagnosis, nor magnitude had absolutely any power over the Answer of healing from God. No alleged sin determined worthiness for healing. Healing was granted on faith alone.

Was the Resurrection Necessary?

Jesus gave countless examples of healing many types of infirmaries to strengthen our faith in God's love and power within us so we would denounce the ego's (inner critic's) claims. In spite of all the miracles he performed, there was yet tremendous doubt and fear among those who had explicitly witnessed these miracles. What more could Jesus have done to convince us of our divine protection, but to use an extreme situation such as the resurrection?

The resurrection was meant to demonstrate the truth about death, the ultimate human fear. He knew we feared death the most of all human experiences. Because of a strong fear of death, it was necessary to demonstrate the eternality of our true Selves (Spirit) through the resurrection.

Our spiritual being (Spirit), which came to experience human form through a conceived body, cannot be destroyed. The body merely houses that spiritual being and obeys its thoughts (instructions).

Was the Resurrection Necessary?

The body's obedience to thought does not give value to the body nor does its manifestation ever transform into that original Spirit. A body merely serves its temporary function defined by its inhabited Spirit. Its obedience to thought instigates its false value since it does not discriminate between incorrect (ego) thoughts or correct thoughts (Spirit). It simply obeys.

The manifestation of those thoughts as illness, aging, etc., strengthens belief in the experience, dismissing a "temporary" purpose for the body. The ego then uses these manifestations to prove to us the "permanent" value of the body. This brings about fear, attack, sin and the need to defend. From this proof, we determine our responses, defined from interpretations, defined from perceptions.

"It is impossible not to believe what you see, but it is equally impossible to see what you do not believe."[10] The interpretation of what we see becomes our perception. Perceptions develop from our experiences and upbringing which then mold our beliefs. Distortion of true perception, that is, when we do not understand what we see, is merely an

interpretation against truth.

For us to say that Jesus suffered would be an ego interpretation. There is nothing written in the books of Matthew, Mark, Luke, or John that he suffered on the cross. Suffering was created through interpretations and strong assumptions of what it must have been like for Jesus during that time on the cross from a human perspective.

The thief beside him accepted forgiveness for his wrongdoings (sins). Sin has different connotations according to our religious upbringing. God does not abandon us even if our decisions look like sin. But when the word "sin" is replaced by error, it reveals unnecessary fear. Fear is not necessary since error is correctable without punishment or suffering.

Some things religions have labeled as sin are not. Often those things are just something which does not adhere to tradition, culture, or man-made laws.

Was the Resurrection Necessary?

In some religions, women are not to expose any part of their body, except their eyes. In some religions, the leader is heavily adorned, while for others they are very plain and simple. For some, material wealth represents great divineness while others feel it creates a separation from God.

These things stem from the belief that our created self can indeed be severed from God's love for us. It is merely an error in thinking for that can only exist in our minds. Acceptance of the error has been corrected through the Atonement. We need do nothing more because the rest has been completed for us through the Atonement that the resurrection gifted us.

The path to peace was made clear and available with the resurrection. It is not a lonely path since everyone who walks on it must bring a brother or sister. Though at first our brother may bring along his errors, he will correct them with our support, and then join us in the resurrection of our inherent eternality, power, and salvation.

Chapter 12 – Exercise:

Write down:

1. List 3 practices of a religion outside of yours that you think are not good.
2. Explain why for each one.
3. Write down what you think would be a good correction to it.
4. How will your correction make the followers lives better?
5. What do you know about that religion's culture?
6. What do they know about your religion's culture?
7. What do you know about the origins of your beliefs that support your corrections to another religion?

13

Wizard of Oz

a metaphysical interpretation

"We often have dark moments when things seem threatening and terrifying. On our journey, we may encounter darkness with no apparent way around it. Sometimes it is through the seeming darkness that we reach our goal." – Helen Gordon

The Wizard of Oz, a 100-year old story, demonstrates many of the principles of A Course In Miracles (the Course), a teaching of judgment, enemies, love, and forgiveness. Author Lyman Frank Baum (1856-1919), provides an entertaining example using the orphan, Dorothy Gale.

In this metaphysical interpretation, sometimes I include metaphysical terminology in parenthesis, next to words or phrases for better understanding. Although this interpretation is meant to clarify teachings of the Course, it also provides insight into how we may perceive our relationships with others.

The 1939 movie version of the Wizard of Oz story begins where Dorothy was frantic that her dog, Toto, would be taken away or harmed as a result of his behavior. She found excuses for him in spite of his destructive behavior. Toto chased Miss Almira Gulch's cat and trampled her flowers whenever they passed her house.

Miss Gulch, of little patience, threatened Dorothy and Toto each time they passed by her house. In Dorothy's mind, she had a monumental problem with Miss Gulch and no one cared to help her resolve it; everyone seemed oblivious to her pain. Psychologists might refer to it as negative attention.

Desperately, she wanted someone, anyone, to agree that her choice was not due to her own misconduct. In Dorothy's mind, her innocence was being ignored by everyone. She insisted that change needed to come from Miss Gulch (projection of guilt), not her.

Hunk, one of the workers at her Uncle's farm offered a good simple solution, *"Don't go past Miss Gulch's house!"*

Here was a very simple solution to Dorothy's problem, the power to create a peaceful relationship with Miss Gulch. Dorothy could not see that she herself was the problem. She had been warned many times of Toto's unacceptable behavior and its ramifications, but insisted on exercising her "right" to walk past Miss Gulch's house. How much trouble would it have been for her peace of mind, as well as for Miss Gulch, to choose another route? Dorothy could have chosen to allow peace instead of chaos. Too often, the ego convinces us to choose the defiant path to prove a useless point.

Training Toto could have mended the relationship too. However, she considered herself the victim to a mean and cruel person.

Rather than change her route (change her mind), Dorothy ran away from home to escape the dreadful problem no one seemed to care about, which was the threat of separation from her dear Toto (source of love) and only friend.

Some of us run away literally, while others run to drugs, alcohol, or other temporary mental escapes from what seems to be a hopeless unloving situation or separation from love. We avoid taking responsibility for creating the love we desire.

On her journey to nowhere, Dorothy met Professor Marvel, a traveling magician. He pretended to read her future using a crystal ball and provided a false prediction to purposely frighten her to return home. The magician appealed to her emotion (ego) and guilt to influence her return home. It worked, for she frantically headed back home with Toto in tow.

The journey back home was a frightening one for Dorothy as a storm approached. Nothing was stable, nothing seemed safe. Horrified, she ended up facing an enormous tornado, and then life got out of control.

First, she headed for safety, pulled at the storm door, but it would not open. Desperately, she ran to the house and rushed through her bedroom door; an object struck her head and she fell unconscious. She symbolically had lost her way home, separated from the family she loved, and entered a dream state as the

Wizard of Oz

house spun furiously in the eye of the tornado (confused and overwhelmed by life's turmoil).

Now, the Course says that we have merely fallen asleep and only need to awaken from the dream. In Dorothy's dream, she found herself in an imaginary world, Oz. This becomes her reality and world of victimization.

Her new life of victimization first began in Munchkin Land, where her wildly spinning house fatally landed on the Wicked Witch of the East. In appreciation of this fatality, which ended wicked control, Dorothy mysteriously found herself instantly wearing the dead witch's ruby red slippers.

Although killing the wicked witch ended evil in Munchkin Land, Dorothy's guilt emerged for murdering the witch. The ego drastically discounted her success. She held on to this guilt in spite of having brought peace and joy to the land. The Course says that guilt seeks punishment and finds it. And plenty of it comes her way.

Glenda, the good witch, appeared and explained the value of Dorothy's red slippers. From a metaphysical perspective, these slippers represented her intuitive guidance, protection, and power over all things, obstacles, and situations. She could surely find her way back home.

All Dorothy wanted was to get back to Kansas (home) and so began the whole story of her journey back home. She had wanted to leave her home in Kansas so badly, but after achieving it, all she could think of was returning home.

The good witch warned her, *"Never ever take those ruby slippers off your feet for a moment or you are at the mercy of the Wicked Witch of the West."* It is similar to *remembering* your power, do not lose sight of it, or try to give it away, lest you fall under the influence of the ego.

The good witch sent her off to find the Wizard of Oz in Emerald City, who would have the directions for her way back home. *"How do I start to Emerald City?"* Dorothy asked. *"It's always best to start at the beginning,"* said Glenda. The beginning was right where Dorothy stood. She just had to get started on the path of her dreams, the yellow brick road, and then follow it.

Getting started can be a challenge when we are paralyzed by fear or indecisiveness (another form of fear). A mere start, regardless of momentum, is what will eventually help you reach a goal. The yellow brick road can symbolize the right guidance of the Holy Spirit. It will lead us where we want to go if we but follow it. As a brick road, it becomes a physical form to help us remain focused and to stay on course. For on the road to Truth, we learn many lessons, create many new relationships, and victor many challenges.

Various characters in the movie too were seeking outside themselves for things considered critical to feeling complete. They felt incomplete, that somehow they were lacking in some area. These things became their issues. Life would have no joy without these things.

The Course says we lack nothing. We have all we need, right within us. It is just being denied. Denial dictates we seek gurus, rituals and things to help us get rid of our lack. When these things fail, they are deemed the cause of our lack and validate our claim to the reality and power of our issues.

Scarecrow (hung up)

Have you found yourself hung up on something that is holding you back?

Scarecrow believed, "*I am a failure because I have no brain.*" He declared he was a victim and mockery of the crows. Victimization was his excuse for ignorance. This was an attempt to project his failure onto the crows through blame. His stupidity and failure in his career were not his fault. The crows were deemed proof of his alleged failure, uselessness and hopelessness. Too often, what the bullies say about us is allowed to become our reality. The taunts become our inner voice and our excuse for how we respond to or not respond to life.

Being bullied was Scarecrow's excuse for his ignorance. He declared he was a victim, bullied by the crows. This was an attempt to project his failure onto the crows through blame. Blame was used to prove that his stupidity and failure in his job to protect the crop were not his fault. The crows were deemed proof of his alleged failure, uselessness and hopelessness of his future.

With very little self-confidence, Scarecrow asked Dorothy, "*Do you think the Wizard will give me a brain?*" She responded, "*I don't know, but even if he didn't, you wouldn't be worse off.*" Often we are afraid to do something we desire for fear of failure. Usually, there is nothing to lose and the only sure way to success is a try. Scarecrow joins her.

On the other hand, was Scarecrow's question referring to worthiness? This is never an issue. As the Course says, "*It is that you ask for far too little.*" Your worth was established by God. You only need to accept God's high value of you.

Scarecrow was the worker, Hunk, on the farm in Kansas. Hunk came up with the logical solution to Dorothy's relationship with Miss Gulch.

Hunk: "*Now look it, Dorothy. You ain't usin' your head about Miss Gulch. Think you didn't have any brains at all!*"

Dorothy: "*I have so got brains.*"

Hunk: "*Well, why don't you use 'em? When you come home, don't go by Miss Gulch's place. Then Toto won't get in her garden, and you won't get in no trouble, see?*"

Dorothy: "*Oh, Hunk. You just won't listen, that's all.*"

Tin Man (stuck in the same place, stagnant)

Further along the yellow brick road, Dorothy and Scarecrow encounter an unclear faint cry for help. How often do we want to cry out for someone to help us, but have difficulty expressing it? We clam up for so long, that it becomes difficult to speak. We just cannot get the words out on our own.

After listening intently they both realize that the Tin Man had rusted and could not move his mouth to speak. In fact, his whole body was immobile. The thing Tin Man needed most to gain his freedom, an oil can, was just inches away from his grasp. (How close are we to our burning desires?) Dorothy grabbed it and lubricated Tin Man's joints, which gave him free movement and freedom to speak.

Tin Man felt, "*If only I had a heart*, then...." He had the "If only" blues. Oh how much he could do; oh what he could be "if only......" He was depressed, deep in self-pity, paralyzed by his belief that what he had was not enough. These are emotions that devastate the heart, creating a host of stress-related diseases.

Tin Man was the worker, Hickory, at the farm. He was working on a metal instrument when interrupted by the commotion of Dorothy falling into the pig sty.

Here we have the brainless Scarecrow who *thought* about going to the Wizard and the emotionless Tin Man who was *depressed*, both claiming they did not have what they sought from the Wizard. Each was so much into their own victimization and shortcomings that they did not even see the truth for each other. So off they all went to see the Wizard.

Dorothy, Scarecrow, and Tin Man merrily skipped down the yellow brick road where they inevitably had to pass through a dark and creepy forest (a little darkness in life). They did not like this darkness; it was frightening. Surely something wicked lurked in the darkness waiting to harm them.

We often have dark moments, moments when things seem threatening and terrifying. On our journey, we may encounter darkness with no apparent way around it. Sometimes it is through the seeming darkness that we reach our goal.

As they walked through darkness, one thing the Scarecrow said while they were in the dark and creepy forest was, "*It will get darker before lighter.*"

However, there was nothing on that dark and creepy portion of the journey that would have or could have hurt them. Couldn't have told them that at one point when the ferocious Lion leaped out to block their path. We know what horrible things a Lion can do! After all, he is the king of the jungle! Says so in the encyclopedia (it's a fact). Lions are not friendly and are known to devour intruders we are told.

Lion (terrified boaster, bully)

Just like the ego, Lion was just an all-talk bully. He boasted and growled, trying to frighten everyone, hiding behind his cowardly facade. People will appear in life, hiding their cowardice with boasts, aggression, intimidation, and put-downs. If you know any lions in your life, face them.

Lion confronted each one, got in their face, and then verbally put them down harshly. He needed to destroy their belief in themselves to make himself look more powerful. This verbal abuse toward his victims was what he really believed to be true about himself.

At first, Scarecrow, Tin Man and Dorothy were terrified by his words and accepted what he said to be truth. They believed they were those awful things he claimed.

We do not have to accept anyone's opinion of us. It is only an opinion, which cannot change who we truly are. Bro. Ishmael Tetteh asks, *"How can you allow your life to be run by opinions of people who themselves do not now why they have those opinions?"*

Dorothy found courage amidst her fear and stood up to Lion! When something she valued was threatened, she fought back. She let go of her fears for an instant to face the dangerous challenge! Lion backed down.

We too only need to find the courage to stand up against those challenges that seem surely to beat us, consume us, or kill us. Remember, we are always wearing those ruby slippers, determined to find our way back home. The Holy Spirit is always guiding us when we commit to following the safe yellow brick road.

Sometimes we question our worthiness of this guidance. Lion questioned his worthiness to join the trio when they invited him to come along to find courage for himself. He responded, *"Wouldn't you be embarrassed to be in the company of a cowardly lion?"*

This is comparison and signs of low self-esteem. It is the not-good-enough song we may hear humming in our ears from time to time. People often accuse others of not respecting their worth, when it is really their own judgment about themselves.

Being king of the jungle, there were expectations of a lion described in his encyclopedia that Lion knew he would not be able to fulfill. An animal researcher of sorts had defined a lion's demeanor and capabilities; therefore, it was a fact in the Lion's coward mind. This confirmed for Lion that he had failed his role.

After Scarecrow and Dorothy convinced Lion to seek courage from the Wizard, they all merrily continued the journey to Oz, skipping down the yellow brick road. They were all pumped up and very hopeful.

Dorothy, always being the positive one, encouraged the others that they too could obtain their dreams. They were "hoping" she was right.

They traveled that yellow brick road on *Dorothy's* faith, not their own.

This is okay. She held the light of truth for them. We need each other in that respect, someone to hold the light for us or someone who can see the light for us, so we can stay on the path of our goal. At a point, we will see the light for ourselves.

Lion was Zeke, the courageous one who saved Dorothy when she fell into the pig sty at the farm. He was quite shaken as he pulled her out of that muddy sty.

Zeke (to the pigs): *"Say, get in there before I make a dime bank outta ya!"*

(To Dorothy) *"Are you gonna let that ol' Gulch heifer buffalo ya? She ain't nothin' to be afraid of. Have a little courage, that's all."*

Wicked Witch of the West (what's out to get you)

Further along the journey, they ran into the wicked witch of the West, alleged proof that there are powers to which they were weak and helpless.

How could they possibly reach their goal with something so powerfully evil against them? With greed, the wicked witch was determined to get even more power by taking the ruby slippers from Dorothy. But we do not need to give up our power to that which threatens us, especially to something or someone so powerless.

Dorothy even tried to give the ruby slippers to the wicked witch, but even Dorothy could not remove them from her own feet. We can deny our power, but it can never be given away.

We can deny who we are, but we cannot change who we are, which are powerful beings. We can deny the love of God, but we cannot be without it. Those shoes were her divine protection and guidance to the love and home she thought was lost forever.

But how could they conquer this most evil and powerful thing (witch)? It was a simple, intuitive response that worked. Water, the source of life, what seemed to be no weapon at all, was what killed the evil witch. This was a simple and readily available tool. It always existed; the right method simply had not been applied until then.

Miss Gulch was seen riding her bike in the tumultuous sky as terrified Dorothy looked out the window of the spinning house. She is the Wicked Witch of the West riding a broom in Oz who was out to get Dorothy. Dorothy took this alleged victimization into her imaginary world.

It Was Always There

Throughout this journey, their determination supported the skills they already possessed. Brainless Scarecrow concocted clever ways to move beyond obstacles that led to ultimately killing the wicked witch who had blocked their path to the Wizard. Heartless Tin Man worried about Dorothy while cowardly Lion frightened away intruders.

Finally, they arrived at Emerald City but were devastated when they met the fake Wizard. After such a long treacherous journey, they discovered that what they were seeking outside of themselves (Wizard) was no more powerful than they.

Wizard recognized the truth about them and proceeded to reveal their capabilities to them in a tangible form they could proudly recognize and accept.

Scarecrow was given a diploma. It was merely a piece of paper acknowledging he had a brain. It did not require a transplant. There was no void to fill. That piece of paper was what convinced Scarecrow that he "finally had a brain."

Upon acceptance of this written intellectual confirmation (diploma), Scarecrow then blurted out the Pythagorean Theorem. That mathematical theorem was always in his head (brain). Faith in himself, strengthened by written acknowledgment, just allowed his exceptional intelligence to come forth.

Next, Wizard pinned a large impressive medal of courage on Lion. That simple medal convinced Lion that he could do anything and fear nothing! He too had tangible proof acknowledging his tremendous courage.

Tin Man cried often throughout the journey, often rusting his joints. Yet it was not until the Wizard handed him a heart shaped ticking clock that he was convinced he had a heart. The clock ticked (beat) as a heart. Again, more physical proof of what already existed within.

Each one of them always had what they were seeking: intellect, courage and love. All of these talents also existed in each of them. Abilities were always being demonstrated, but they had not noticed for hopelessly blaming, denying and focusing on what they could **not** do. So much so that they believed they could not. Their abilities had been concealed by self-pity and attitudes of defeat.

Dorothy's turn came to get what she was seeking, to float home in the repaired hot-air balloon with the Wizard. While busy attending to others and searching for Toto, she missed her take-off and believed that was her last chance to get back home. Devastated, she watched her dream drift away.

How often do we think we have missed our last chance at something, missed qualifying by a few points on an exam, missed a deadline, or miscalculated? New opportunities will never cease to greet us. These are only thoughts of lack and limitation. There is no limit to the power of God and no last opportunity exists.

There is no one way of doing something, no one way to reach the goal. Yet we often limit our vision of how something should be achieved, never looking for another way to obtain it. We grieve over the seeming loss and stare hopelessly at our balloon (opportunity) adrift without us and ask, "Why me?"

Also, Dorothy's last minute frantic search for Toto and her emotional goodbyes of regret for leaving friends behind, represent hesitation to grasp opportunity she had worked very hard to get. This was not the way she had envisioned her return home.

In the midst of Dorothy's moment of self-pity and seeming hopelessness, the beautiful Good Witch appeared. The others asked the Good Witch why Dorothy did not get what she wanted when everyone else did. The good witch answered, "It was not enough to want."

When the Good Witch asked Dorothy what she had learned, Dorothy replied, *"If ever I go looking for my heart's desire again, I won't go further than my own back yard (within me). Because if it isn't there, it was never lost to begin with."* All we need is within us. Right where we are is the answer. We are always at home.

The others asked why she was sent to the Wizard when that was all she had to know. The Good Witch responded, *"She had to learn (do the work) it for herself."*

This book presents simple ideas and principles that work but are difficult to believe that healing is that easy. Also, this book does not lead us to outside sources for emotional healing; it guides us to using our own minds, thoughts and power.

As with Dorothy, we may hesitate at the opportunities that lead us to our goals for fear of leaving something or someone we value behind, or feel we need to give up (sacrifice) something.

We refer to those things as sacrifices we are not willing to make. Dorothy did not need to sacrifice anything real to board the balloon. She only had to relinquish her valuables in form and fantasy in exchange for reality which had everything she wanted.

Yes, it may be difficult to ignore the seeming danger when the witch is scowling in our faces. The witch deliberately does this because it knows that the bigger the fear, the weaker the person.

To keep our power, we must control the fear. Fear control helps to make decisions for intelligent planning. Anger control makes for executing the plan successfully. We can go home, travel to anywhere, or achieve whatever we desire.

We are all Dorothy and her friends. We have the courage, brains, love and power to find our way home, to reach our goals, and to live our dreams. Keep wearing those ruby slippers. As the Course says, we are merely trying to find our way back home to heaven. Use the yellow brick road (inner guidance) to find it.

Dorothy woke up from her injury, grateful to find that she was at home--in her bed, surrounded by love, not enemies. It all seemed so real, yet it had all been a dream of a journey to Oz, to find her way back home.

In that moment of awakening, Dorothy realized that each person at that Kansas farm had played a role in her dream, disguised as a different character (past life). Only their form had changed. All of them had always loved her and wanted the best for her. With her awakening, she recognized their love for her. She could appreciate them just the way they were, each with their own needs and ways of living life.

The journey was all an illusion with lessons for inner growth. It all seemed so real and at times things seemed threatening, unfair, or hopeless. She had lost everything but Toto. Now, she had to face the witches of this new world.

Those things only existed in her created fantasy in her world of Oz. All the while, she had never left home but in her mind. Strength she did not know she had, got her to the Wizard and eventually back home.

> This chapter goes into more detail in *The Obvious Secret Lesson of the Wizard of Oz – a metaphysical interpretation of "A Course in Miracles."* It reveals hidden meanings behind the balloon, apple, water, oil can, flower field, castle door, wind, pig sty, etc. It provides an even closer look at yourself.

Chapter 13 – Exercise:

Identify persons you have interacted with as you traveled your yellow brick road of life.

1. Name your wicked witch (three or less, male and/or female).
2. What do they have in common? (if more than one wicked witch)
3. What did you learn from the relationship(s)?
4. What was good about the relationship(s)? Although you may find it difficult, look for even the smallest good.
5. Name your good witch (four or less)
6. List their similar traits and contributions to your sanity.
7. Who has been heavily dependent upon you for their success or happiness? (name three)
8. Have you sacrificed your own success for theirs?
9. List your traits, habits or thoughts similar to Dorothy's.
10. What love do you fear losing?
11. List on paper **at least one** trait or habit you have that is similar to each character in the story. Examples are in parenthesis.
    a. Wicked witch (vindication, temper,) jealousy, envy, power struggle, control, etc.).

b. Good witch (caring, wise, mentor)
c. Munchkin (someone dependent upon you).
d. Scarecrow (intellectually challenged or embarrassed, hung up on some negative belief).
e. Lion (afraid, aggressive boastful, bully).
f. Tin Man (procrastinates, paralyzed, makes no progress, numb, and out of shape).
g. Wizard (problem solver, a shoulder to others, façade, guru).
h. Toto (loving, promiscuous, or breaks rules, defiant).
i. Aunt Em (nurturing, straight-laced, workaholic, serious)
j. Miss Gulch (lack patience, closed minded, begrudging, condemning).

14

Reclaim Your Self-Esteem

"If you go beyond mediocrity, mediocrity won't like you." – Dr. Michael Beckwith

"Too often we are more afraid of losing someone's love than we are of losing ourselves." – Helen Gordon

What do we think of ourselves? What do we think we are worth? What do we think we deserve in life? These answers define our world and our approach to it.

Self-esteem is subtly influenced by this world. What goes into creating that world has also influenced who we think we are, what we think we are worth, who we think we should be and what kind.

As children, we remembered certain adult conversations, especially those of our parents. Repetitious responses to certain things stuck with us. We incorporated them as our own, or accepted that what our parents did was surely the proper response to life. Children are very impressionable during those early years. Before our teenage years, what our parents said or believed was held as sacred truth.

Have you ever heard a small child innocently repeat something characteristic of a certain adult? The quote is amusingly exact. It is one of few times we happen to be aware that the child was listening to that adult. They have been remembering more than the phrases they dare repeat. What else of that person or other adults will he or she mock?

Sometimes as children we listened curiously to gossip or debates; we watched the reactions of the adults. Curiously, we watched what had favorable reactions and which ones were unfavorable. From this we learned our own manipulation skills, what was adored, what won friends, and what behavior just absolutely was not acceptable.

Watching is a subtle and impressionable means of learning for children. They put into action what looks "cool," fun, and especially acceptable in their community and among their peers. This is the first stage of creating habit and seeking acceptance. The need for acceptance is strong.

The belief is if we look cool, we have a stronger chance at being accepted. Valuing acceptance also seems to be learned, the cooler the better. What looks like cool for our particular peers varies. If we look fun, we will be accepted. Everyone will want to be around us and love us. We have seen that work for Mr. /Ms. Popular.

If we do not have the skills or confidence to be cool or fun, there is physical acceptance that can override those shortcomings we think. When all else fails, academic smarts just might draw acceptance status. Most energy is used toward being accepted in some way, even in adulthood.

Socially we have been taught that wall-flowers are rejected, so we must avoid being one. We are taught that a less than ideal body will bring about intimate and social rejections. Low intellectual levels bring about many exclusions and cruel bullying.

Social and intellectual inadequacies are considered shortcomings. These shortcomings have been defined while listening to gossip, debates, and television shows. As we learn to camouflage some or all of these alleged shortcomings, we remain in constant fear of being exposed lest the horrid rejection consume our lives. Commitment to this façade will begin to feel real, forgetting it was made up. This makes it more difficult to see that the rejection is not toward us but to the facade and dishonesty it represents.

Confusion happens when rejection occurs on that insane level. It feels like punishment; therefore, we must have sinned. If we have sinned then we are guilty. Guilty?!! Sinned?!!! Shhhhh! What if someone finds out? We cannot remember what the sin was, but whatever it was, we must hide it or we have no way out of this punishment and rejection.

Although we are not sure what it is we have done, we commence to do whatever it takes to hide this alleged sin. We cannot bear to see what it is; we become terrified of this unknown. It could be any of those horrible things we heard mentioned in gossip conversations, what the minister spoke condemningly about in church, or something that could ruin our family heritage, inheritance or reputation. Somehow, a substantial loss is destined to occur and we fear we will be "the blame."

Blame is associated with being *responsible* for or the *cause of* something negative. Sin is not something we want to be responsible for because we were taught that it brings nothing but destruction, pain, rejection, isolation and worst of all, hell. How could we face such a responsibility?

Since we have been sentenced to hell-fire and cannot bear the thought day after day, we resort to denial as a protection mechanism for our conscious mind and hopefully as a pardon of our sins or reconsideration for heaven. Denial becomes our savior. Anything threatening its existence and function in our lives will be attacked with a vengeance.

Denial becomes habit, a way of life, totally unnoticed for what it has become; we have been doing it for so long.

So many years pass that we do not even remember why we started hiding in the first place and surely do not remember the "sin" we allegedly committed. Well no wonder we do not remember it, there never was a sin, just a self-condemnation.

However, this created condemnation now has control over our lives. It seeks punishment and anything that does not resemble peace or forgiveness.

Slowly it continues to destroy our self-worth. In the event we find ourselves experiencing peace, the ego voice will remind us that we do not deserve the gift because of our sinful secret; therefore, let it go for someone who does deserve it. This is self-sabotage, yet we resent those who respond to receive the gift (worthiness) we have chosen to pass to them as being more worthy.

Most of us are guilty of nothing more than a thought or suspicion. Some are guilty according to a cultural, social or religious belief. It is not guilt, just a difference in opinion of how we should conduct our lives or make choices.

Some have mastered denial and know no other way of survival. It is not enjoyable. In fact, it is quite complicated. Nevertheless, it is familiar and comfortable to some extent.

Having no denial means facing too many terrifying unknowns. Perhaps these unknowns we think could be harmful. We ask, "What will they think?; what if we are 'found out?'; or what will God say?"

What others think about us controls our every move. Rejection becomes a threat too close to our fragile little happiness if "they" knew the truth about us; we believe that no one would love us.

We desperately hold on to our created means of controlling or receiving the only love we know, regardless of how painful it has become. If we change now, we will not be loved at all we think. There is great fear of losing love. We have experienced the pain of not being loved and by golly, we have particular people we are not going to take that chance with. If we have to do some rejecting ourselves, we will, to keep our special loves.

There is not much choice that we can see. We must remain in control of that love. It is not much but it is all we have or all we seem to deserve.

Are we obsessed with losing the love of someone more than we are of losing ourselves? If we lose ourselves, **that** is the greatest loss of love. It is a denial of the Love from which we were created. More value is placed on our ego-created love than true Love.

Self-love is not selfish, it is loving God. It is a gesture of gratitude for the love, which can be expressed through us and for us. When we accept self-love, we are freer to give love without obligation, fear or remorse. It does not control us or define our worth.

We are learning from this book to bring out those elements of our being that override those fears. We learn that we know we can win against any challenge. Also, this book helps us to see beyond the situation or circumstance, and not put ourselves on hold until it "looks right" to go on, until it is "safe" to go on, or when we are sure we can do this or that.

Always waiting for the right time? Wait no more! It is time to do what we can do. The more we do it, the better we are at it. As we improve, our confidence will build and we will demonstrate how invincible we are. Nothing and no one will or can determine our strength and ability to succeed. All we need is given to us at birth. This is the Truth. It cannot change. We are dependent on no one but our own thoughts.

By catching a bit of someone else's belief in us, when we do not believe in ourselves, we can build from their faith. Eventually that faith becomes ours.

This chapter's exercise can help us with inner house cleaning so we can find where we have hidden our self-esteem. As we find it or it becomes visible, do not deny it for error cannot hurt us; however, ignoring it can.

Allow the correction to happen. Our lives depend on it. Take small steps towards this goal. **Every** step is certainly closer. Anywhere we go, regardless how fast, it takes one step at a time to reach the goal. Sometimes we slice it up like pie in different sizes then call it several steps. Slice it the way is most supportive, but slice! See the correction as the dessert of life.

How to start? With the mind first! All corrections should start there, whatever the goal. Start with the mind. As we change our minds, so will self-esteem.

We are still worn and tired, and the desert's dust still seems to continuously blind our eyes and keep us sightless. *"Only a little wall of dust still stands between you and joy."*[11] Blow on it lightly with happy laughter, and it will fall away more and more with each breath.

Chapter 14 - Exercise:

1. Name three people who have told you what you are worth.
2. Do you believe them?
3. Whom do you agree with? Why?
4. The next opportunity someone offers that you go first in a line, do it. Respond with a simple, Thank You and not a word more. The ego will chatter, but do it anyway. It's time for **you** to acknowledge your worth.
5. Buy three of your favorite fruits and a melon. Make a fruit salad. Take out your fancy dishes and put a helping on it. Enjoy it. Do this each day until you run out of fruit. Be mindful of the taste of your fruit salad. How does it taste? If there is any negative chatter, what is it telling you? If you do not have a fancy dish, go out and buy just one small fancy crystal bowl, new or used.

15

Sacrifice is Not Necessary

"Suppressed resentment can build from too much sacrificing regardless how innocent the intention." – Helen Gordon

What have you gained from sacrifice? What value does it hold for you? Sacrifice says that something of value must be given up in order to gain something else. Often it is something that is used to measure love *from* or *for* another in some form. A bargaining of some kind is required to purchase this love or swap some for more or equal value, according to personal criteria.

Some sacrifices become a determination of self-worth. They are made as an unconscious installment to insure no loss of love from someone. It is intended to elevate the sacrificer's worth through some martyr act or hopefully heal their past.

Sacrifice Is Not Necessary

If love, worth, or healing are not satisfied as envisioned, there is great disappointment in whom or for what the sacrifice offered. When the outcome or response is not as the ego required, attack by labeling others seems necessary. Others are labeled ungrateful and selfish, "after-all-you-have-done" (sacrificed) to prove your worthiness of another's affection. Feelings of humiliation and victimization surface, not love. By golly, that sacrifice should have generated showers of love!

Our self-worth did not improve. What we were trying to change about ourselves, the situation, or someone else appears either unchanged or worse than before. Subsequently, we become angry with ourselves for having failed that attempt, and then try to project the guilt of failure on to our alleged victimizer. This way, blame for the failure and unloving response is no longer ours. Innocence is believed to have been re-established while the guilt was projected onto the victimizer.

As long as the person(s) or circumstance(s) responds as we expect, we will continue to gladly make sacrifices, that is, the sacrifice is conditional and binding. This expected response is according to expectations secretly set forth in our minds. Others either know nothing of these expectations or find it impossible to fulfill them to our standards. This is our investment in the relationship where a favorable reciprocation of sorts is sought.

Sacrifice will always be painful in this case because it has self-defined expectations. A sacrifice is never done for nothing. We place value on the response because it determines how loved we are or proves our love, which in turn is used to measure our worth. Other times it may be used to prove a judgment we have against someone.

Occasionally, this judgment is intended to prove how better a person we are than another or supports an opinion of some kind. We have something to prove that seems worth the cost. Perhaps it will even increase our popularity (worth). There is power in popularity we think because we can now influence those who love us.

A sacrifice says, "I am acting out of love so if you do not respond with love or reject my sacrifices (my solicitation for love), either you do not love me or I do not matter to you. My love is not valuable so I am not valuable. I am deeply hurt and feel rejected!" Rejection attacks the body as illness, which the ego claims is further physical proof we are not loved.

A gift can be given without sacrifice when it is given without expectation of any kind. When a gift is no longer a sacrifice, it is healthy. The gift is then allowed to bless all involved.

Suppressed resentment can build from too much sacrificing regardless how innocent the intention. Resentment also attacks the body, which is an expression of anger against oneself. The inner critic nags that we have not done enough and shoves guilt into our minds.

Repeatedly we attempt to pass the guilt to someone else, yet we still feel enormous guilt. We are not satisfied. In fact, the guilt seems more burdensome now and greater effort to get rid of it becomes necessary and exhausting. The subconscious mind knows of the guilt and tells the body it must be punished.

Sacrifice Is Not Necessary

The body obeys the thought since it can make no decision on its own. Illness or adverse situations are then attracted to the body to satisfy this demand of punishment. Having no control to decide on its own, the body accepts the attack.

The ego has disguised the punishment to appear external, uncontrollable, real, and indirect. Yet, guilt is indeed self-punishment. No one else has anything to do with it. It was a choice made solely in our minds; therefore, it is controllable and optional. We determine the degree of punishment. Self-infliction can only be direct. There are no prosecutors but us. It is a lone act of self-crucifixion.

Sacrifice costs true peace, joy, and health. How much have you invested in an attempt to receive these gifts?

Any sacrifice is an attempt to receive these gifts either for ourselves or for someone else. These gifts are actually limited because of sacrifice. The amount received is determined either by the amount of sacrifice defined in our minds or as defined through cultural, religious, social, or geographic rules. These rules portion the gifts according to its criteria.

When we allow God to determine our limitless gifts, we open up to the world to receive limitless blessings. Eliminate the words, "too much" from thoughts and conversations when it comes to blessings and good that can be received. The Father knows how much we are ready to handle. Our charge is to prepare for a full cup of good life, refillable at any time and without sacrifice.

Chapter 15 - Exercise:

Create a vision board

1. What would you like to receive without sacrifice? Strong belief that you can have it will come later.
2. Cut out pictures that reflect just that, and then paste them onto a poster board. Dare to dream big!
3. Each morning, simply look at each picture on the board.
4. Repeat step 3 each evening.
5. Make adjustments to the board, by replacing new photos sometimes, but only replace them with "better ones" that portray your desires more clearly.

16

Avoiding the Holiday Blues

"Now is the season to change our thinking."
– Helen Gordon

Holiday seasons can be the least joyous on occasion. It would be nice to fast forward through them sometimes. There are many expectations around the holidays be it social, religious, cultural, or monetary. Happy holidays are measured by how well the expectations of it are met. These expectations are probably inherited, self-created, or socially defined for us.

Once it has come to a point where we dread the holidays, then it is time to abandon these expectations and **be** the happy person we can be. We can experience the good times we have always desired and enjoy the holidays to the fullest.

Being a holiday victim is no fun. People will begin to avoid such victims for fear of them affecting their holiday merriment. They fear the victim's lack of joy is contagious.

Regardless of when we are reading this, now is the season to change our thinking. Bring on the cheer! Depend not upon things and people to make it so for that is a trap of the ego, which captures its prey every time.

A conscious positive change in thoughts will attract positive events. Discard old expectations to begin drawing glad tidings to the holiday celebration.

Each person has their own set of expectations planned for the holiday's activities. Expectations are how we have continued to create disappointment during the holidays. A holiday is labeled as a bad holiday if these expectations are not met. Habitual bad holidays are simply an unconscious attraction of things to validate this negative occurrence as destiny and to mold this one to be no different than those of the past.

In an attempt to defy the past, financial sacrifices are made which can cause dreadfully high monetary commitments that can last for years. Each sacrifice is meant to serve as an installment for a happy holiday.

When is it a sacrifice? If we cannot comfortably afford the cost of something, it is a sacrifice. Cost can be time, money, or energy. The form does not matter. Sacrifice is neither necessary nor valuable. However, expectations tend to become more valuable and very meaningful where sacrifice is involved. This applied value makes it more difficult to release the expectation because its alleged value justifies it and supports the need to sacrifice.

Holidays are not a time for sacrifice. Instead, it is a time to give without sacrifice. Sacrifices may be to meet an obligation, to impress, or to seek love. Anything given to satisfy an obligation, to receive something in return, or to obtain love, is not a gift; it is the ego's pitiful contingent investment in love.

Sometimes these sacrifices unconsciously serve as annual payments for love. Love cannot be purchased or accumulated; only poor replicas of love that do not last are obtained, which is not our true desire.

Year after year, sacrifices have been an attempt to assure a dear one's material happiness. Surely all we have done in the name of love will be socially recognized we think; surely it will be appreciated and returned, at least partially. At least some attempt to demonstrate gratitude and love toward us is expected. Maybe it will happen this holiday season we hope.

As we prepare for the holidays, we fantasize about what our neighbors, children, friends, parents, co-workers, in-laws, or spouse will think about our sacrifices **this** time. Holiday party guests (related or not) are assured that nothing more is expected than to simply show up and enjoy what has been prepared.

Once the guests arrive, the expectations dominate our thoughts. Some guests may even share those very thoughts but with their own little twist (their uniqueness). The turkey must be golden, juicy, and picture perfect regardless of the vegetarian guests. Everyone will want to sing our favorite traditional songs when we think it is time. All will be eager to sing their hearts out and love it. Background music of famous crooners of our teen years will be just what **everyone** wants to hear. The teenagers will have no objections.

Each one will just love the perfect gifts we bought for them. Kids will get along well and be perfect little angels. In-laws will be polite. The icing on the cake will be perfect. Not one spill on the rug will happen. Everyone will have the best time and stay sober.

Oh how everyone will marvel at how much we sacrificed for this lovely feast and gift-giving gathering! They will see how thoughtful we were and praise our loving gesture. This is how we want to be remembered, loving and loved. We imagine the good things they will think about us because of the wonderful image we have presented.

Image is very important to us. But what image do we think we have presented to our guests? What will others expect of us after this holiday? We have created **their** expectations with this proudly created image. Since they think the person we presented is who we are and what we are capable of doing, they will expect the same or better next year. Realizing this, we anxiously try to meet that expectation this year too.

Commonly, we create other's expectations of us. Perhaps a pattern or tradition was established in that giving, leading to certain annual expectations of us. It is this image that guests have come to admire. Consequently, they begin to expect a certain behavior from us each year, which we anxiously recognize and accept.

How could we fail to live up to these self-created expectations that have molded an admired image and thus affect our worth? Will our worth to others diminish if we fail? These questions race fearfully through our minds. Therefore, in desperation we strive to preserve this artificial worth through even more sacrifice next time.

This implies a belief that our worth can be altered by sacrifice. How well expectations are met or how much the sacrifice is praised are what we use to measure our worth to our guests.

Worth can never be measured by sacrifice nor altered by a person's opinion. Our worth is not affected by another's response, yet it remains questionable in our minds when the response is not pleasing after all we have given of ourselves.

For years, it seems we have given and received nothing or very little in return. We feel our expectations are not much; just a little appreciation is all we seek to validate the worth we have worked so hard to obtain. These simple expectations seem justified because of all we have done and all we have sacrificed for love.

The ego will say, "It is not too much to expect a thank you, a little recognition, a raise," etc., but it is. It is an expectation nonetheless; something the ego uses to magnify disappointment, determining how "happy" the holiday turned out.

Regardless of seeming significance, when any or all of our expected responses are not received, disappointment will surely follow since this is conditional giving. True giving has no expectations at all. It is completely unconditional from a place of love.

No one needs to validate what we have chosen to do. We simply remain fully satisfied and at peace with our giving.

Chapter 16 - Exercise:

Review your expectations of how the holiday should be celebrated each year

1. How do your expectations support having a happy holiday?
2. Has it worked for your household or guests?
3. Prioritize your expectations, and then let go of one of the top three this year.
4. Let go of any guilt with step 3.
5. Let go of any fear or hesitation when responding to step 3.
6. Observe the inner chatter but do not take what you hear personal.

17

How Do You "Let Go"?

"Surrender is not giving in; it's giving up the things that are not working."

– Iyanla Vanzant

Let go of the drama.

Let go? But how do we do it? We tire of being told at workshop after workshop to "let it go" without any instruction on how to do it. A good place to start is to release the mind of all guilt. Forgive it and let the mind be healed and returned to its wholeness. How do we do this?

Ask for understanding.

Truly ask for understanding, not just for an explanation of why it seems you are being punished or being victimized. Avoid facts to support situations or circumstances claimed to be ruining your life. Before asking for this understanding, put aside any judgments about the situation, any conclusions, and let go of any anxieties, resentments, or grievances around it for a moment. Really clear your mind of any blockages to hear the Answer.

Ask in silence, and then most importantly, listen. Do not judge what you hear during this silence. Release any opinions about it whatsoever. Be determined to do this "let go" thing and let life love you.

Accept the Answer.

From the Answer, there will be something to learn. Understand or learn the lesson put before you. You may not like the lesson, but it either is because you do not fully understand the Answer, resist the Answer, or deny it. If this should occur, take a deep breath and dismiss the session. Try acceptance again another time. Acceptance cannot be forced; it can only be embodied with honest invitation. Once the shift from fear and resistance to acceptance happens, release can happen.

Pray for openness.

Pray for openness and open your inner ears. Try again to accept the Answer if you were not able to in the Acceptance step above. A day or two later, is recommended. When more than two days lapse, the ego will begin to bury your fear of the answer deep in your cellar of resentment where it will emerge as a stress-related discomfort.

How to pray is covered in *There's Nothing Going On But Your Thoughts* Book 1. Obtain a prayer partner and pray together silently whenever possible. Ask friends and acquaintances to pray for you through this journey. Happiness is at hand.

Let the incident go.

Talk it out just once, completely, and with someone neutral, but it need not be rehashed at every subsequent opportunity. Telling your *story* to everyone who will listen is not advisable. The alleged support builds upon the very anger you are trying to release. It is also unhealthy, causing you to re-live the emotion that came up during the incident, aggravating the body's proper functioning.

End the story

Rehashing your drama (*sharing* your story excessively) merely feeds the greed of victimhood as comfort and escape. Nothing more is given to or taken from you or anyone else. You are only weakened and made to hunger for more drama to feed the starving ego.

Repetition of a story is usually indicative of guilt. If you can prove to others that you had nothing to do with the circumstances, you think your innocence will be restored. No person or God will hold it against you. God sees only our innocence.

Deep down, proving our innocence is never satisfied. It is insatiable because you are attempting to fix something that is not broken. You are guilty of nothing and your innocence is unchanged. It was merely an error in thinking which you desire to correct. Allow the Spirit to correct your mind to heal the body.

Spirit rules the mind, which rules the body. Keep this hierarchy in the forefront of all thoughts. Remember this is in all circumstances, situations and events of life. Accept the power of the Spirit and live life fully, allowing this human experience to be enjoyed.

There is no exam or requirement of any kind to pass or fail life and nothing of your past that has the power to prevent your healing but with your allowance. Self-condemnation is what blocks your healing from you. Fortunately, your opinion of yourself is not God's vision of you.

Listen to what the Spirit hears from God, "I love you my child. I will forever love you." Then tell the body just that. And it is not necessary to believe it to do it. Eventually, the mind and your acceptance will catch up; thus, your enlightenment expands.

Chapter 17 - Exercise:

With this exercise, you will learn to relax your mind so that it can let go. Experienced or inexperienced persons can do this exercise with the suggestions at the end of this exercise.

1. Meditate daily for 15 minutes in the morning.
    a. In your pajamas after you have washed your face is best.
    b. Take a question into your Sunday or chosen meditations.
2. Meditate each evening for 15 minutes.
    a. Do this **before** you feel sleepy.
    b. Wear something comfortable (less clothes the better).
    c. Sit in a comfortable chair or on the floor.

Pick one of the following meditation types or alternate the ones you like:

1. Listen to a melody and instruments of a meditative tone or soft classical music. Pick a particular instrument or sound to focus on.
2. Close your eyes and watch your breath. Use ear plugs if your environment has distracting noises.
3. Close your eyes and listen to the wind.

4. Close your eyes and listen to the sounds outside (noisy or not). While your eyes are still closed, look at the space between your eyes.

5. Watch the flickering flame of a candle in a darkened room. Alternate closing your eyes, watching the flame, and blinking.

18

Listening to the Voice

> *"The Voice does not judge our choices but helps us to deal with the results of our choices; It just waits patiently and lovingly for us to ask for help."* – Helen Gordon

Be still an instant to hear the Voice as It speaks in the silence of the mind. The Voice is that which responds to our created reality beyond our perception. Through the Voice, we are physically and emotionally healed, comforted, and divinely guided in all activities. That is Its function.

How do we recognize the Voice?

It often speaks to us in the form of a gut feeling, a hunch, intuition, human instinct, or simply a knowing. Gut feelings seem too easy and mysterious to trust sometimes and it does not feel like we are in control. But the gut feelings *are* what put us in control because it is right guidance. Guidance and answers are why the Voice is available to us when making choices.

There is ***never*** punishment for our choices. Although each choice has a corresponding set of events that may appear as punishment, it is only appearance.

For example, if we choose to touch hot coal, with our bare hands we will experience great pain. Pain is the corresponding event of the law of touching hot coal, not a punishment. Blisters and scaring may also play a part in the outcome.

The Voice does not judge our choices but helps us to deal with the *results* of our choices; It just waits patiently and lovingly for us to ask for help. It is here to support us, but only when invited.

Our listening becomes more automatic as the Voice's sound becomes more recognizable. Though often times we ignore the Voice out of fear, we trust it more with time. We fear the unknown and thus lack faith in our own newly experienced knowledge because we doubt if it is truth or not.

Our minds develop the ability to differentiate between truth and the ego's interpretations as well as recognize God's intent. How would God see this? How would God react? These are questions we learn to ask.

"Understand that you do not respond to anything directly but to your interpretation of it. If you decide that someone is really trying to attack you or desert you or enslave you, you will respond as if he had actually done so, having made his error real to you. ...you react to your interpretations as if you were correct."[12]

"Whatever is in accord with this light He retains, to strengthen the Kingdom in you. A Voice will answer every question you ask, and a vision will correct the perception of everything you see."[13]

This is the Voice, which cannot be heard with ears. It is an inner hearing without mental or physical form. Here is where faith is necessary. The Voice knows what is real in spite of our ego interpretations of life's experiences. It knows the intended purpose of the moment.

How often we have heard, "I'm glad that didn't happen!" We had wished for a certain outcome of a situation, but come to be thankful it did not happen as desired. Life responded to what we had deeply asked for, not what we thought our ego wanted.

We do not trust our seeming little knowledge right now; therefore, the Voice helps us to remember what we already know. We know everything the Voice knows and we are remembering how to access that knowledge. Invite this recollection and it will happen. If the information seems to mock, contradict, or threaten strong beliefs and values learned over the years, be willing to see things differently.

There is a lesson in an interpretation and the Voice turns that into an opportunity to see a situation differently, to see it for what it is, not for what we hope or think we will learn.

What about an experience such as a physical attack? The attack should not be condoned or denied. Most likely it will physically hurt no doubt, but the reason for the attack must still be interpreted through the Voice.

Such an interpretation will make it effortless to forgive, forget, and heal. It may also encourage different future choices so that the situation does not appear in our lives again in any form. Other times it provides a powerful testimony to help others heal.

Often we have told ourselves, "I knew I should not have gone there" or "done that!" The Voice was warning us of an experience we really preferred to skip, but welcomed anyway. Now we have an opportunity to learn, unlearn, or re-learn something. If the interpretation of the experience is from the ego, it will attempt to deny the purpose of that experience by making it seem threatening.

We respond so readily to our interpretation of things, and then believe this interpretation to be so true, so right. Decisions are then based upon this interpretation, declaring the interpretation correct. We may feel comfortable with the wrong interpretation, especially when it satisfies our emotions, but lasting comfort is a by-product of a correct interpretation.

Some wrong interpretations can induce feelings of attack and fear. Children often feel attacked by discipline and thus rebel.

Let us use a rebellious teenage son as an example. When his parents discipline him for choices he makes, his rebellion is based solely upon his interpretation that his parents just do not want him to have fun. They are trying to control his life, take away his identity he claims. The fact is, the parents love him and are only trying desperately to spare him some of life's painful experiences.

He searches angrily within himself for an interpretation of their responses and in his rage, responds unfavorably to his parents. Independence seems threatened, and he fears losing who he thinks he wants to be in the eyes of his friends. In his mind, what his parents are recommending is aimed at separating him from his friends.

Losing his friends means losing acceptance. Losing acceptance means losing love, which threatens his self-esteem and self-worth. Losing love leaves no meaning to life since his parents obviously do not love him either or they would not impose such harsh expectations he thinks.

In desperation, he seeks love by any means available. He blindly grasps at every opportunity not offered by his parents. All of this is because of fear brought about by a communication breakdown due to misinterpretation. When the words do not reflect the action, misinterpretation happens. This is true in any relationship between human beings, be it business, social, intimate, or family.

Before communication degrades to any degree, pray for the words to say that will heal the results of the misinterpretation. Be willing to accept the information the Voice offers you because it may not always fit your idea of a proper response.

Prayer opens our ears so the Voice can be heard for guidance. This opening helps release control to that power greater than our little selves so that we are in full control.

At times we may find ourselves being that teenage son in relationship to the Voice or perhaps with another human being. Join with the Voice to regain inner harmony. Recognize the good and fearful intentions in relationships whether in agreement or not. This will promote clarity yet does not condone negativity or imply agreement with what you discern; it will just interpret the experience to see the Love extended to us or the cry for Love from us.

Chapter 18 - Exercise

Do only one step per day.
1. Close your eyes and reflect on a time when you did not follow a hunch.
   - Capture the emotion of that urging.
   - Observe the fearful inner conversation.
2. Reflect on a time when you followed a hunch and got good results.
   - Capture the emotion of that choice and trust.
   - Observe the fearful inner conversation.
3. Count how many "what-ifs" of the past month really happened.
4. Listen to your hunches this week.
   - Observe your inner conversation.
   - Are there thoughts of *what will they think*?
   - Observe the outcome of your hunch. You need at least 10 of these hunches to have a good observation.
5. How often were your decisions based upon protecting your reputation to any degree or *hoping* things would come out the way you wanted?
6. Step 1 and 2 will help you discern whether the ego or the Voice is speaking to you. Eventually you will recognize the Voice instantly. At times, you may still feel fearful,

but you will be equipped with information to make the right choice.

Step 2 - 5 will help weaken the influence of the ego when making choices. Additionally you will begin to recognize it in others and thus not respond to that ego perception but with love. Trust in your decisions will strengthen your confidence in living life fully and divinely.

19

Pretentious Teacher

"God accepts us on all levels of our understanding along with our self-righteousness, strong opinions, and shortcomings. We have to do the same for others." – Helen Gordon

Sometimes it may be difficult to listen to a speaker who seems pretentious and self-righteous on their spiritual path. Our egos judge them as a bad source of information even though we have no idea what is actually going on inside of them, what their thoughts are, or what experiences positively influence their teaching. What's worse is that our judgment is considered absolute fact about the person and thus creates a separation.

With confidence, we think we know their thoughts and intentions. It is possible to see the ego thoughts and intentions but not the spiritual ones. It is equally irritating when someone thinks they know us better than we do.

Pretentious Teacher

Occasionally we can indeed see someone's potential better than they can. It is disappointing when that person cannot share the same vision. Once they become aware that we see their capabilities, it can be annoying and threatening to them because our insight means they can no longer deny their power with us around. Their denial of their potential is being exposed.

Denial is temporary and never fully effective, thus the pretense must be relinquished at some point. We cannot hide from ourselves or from the truth forever, regardless of the amount of alcohol, drugs, or other thought overrides we use.

Listen to these teachers because they usually have good teachings. I have learned a great deal from some of these teachers. They may not live the truth they are teaching, but the Truth is always the truth whether the speaker is living it or not because we did not create truth.

Often speakers teach from what they have experienced firsthand. We have the ability to go right past the ego to hear what the speaker is saying. Remember, everyone is our teacher. We are also theirs.

In some cases, what the speaker is teaching might incite our anger, which resurrects our own issues, also known as buttons. Those who push our buttons through their alleged facade can cause something to emerge within us that the ego does not want exposed. Ignoring the lesson is being justified by the distraction in the form of *irritation*. Observe it at the next opportunity.

The presentation can be irritating when it brings back a past unpleasant experience with a speaker who presented a similar topic. So we shut out what is currently presented and begin to react to the past presentation, totally muting the voice before us. However, that lesson will repeatedly return until we choose to learn it, since what we resist, persists in our lives. Go ahead; learn the lesson so this experience will finally go away. Then we can move forward easier on our spiritual journey.

How do we counter someone who thinks our spiritual journey and all related books we read are incorrect? We don't. Why fight the ego? Living the Truth each day will be enough example for them. Just have them watch, listen, and read for themselves. Understand that they have a choice in their own interpretation because they do. We will surely have ours! Let them have their opinion too. In any given moment people are doing the best they can as unbelievable as it sometimes appears.

God accepts us on all levels of our understanding along with our self-righteousness, strong opinions, and shortcomings. Do the same for others. We are no better than God. To place our "standards" and acceptance criteria more strict than God's is silly. This does not mean to accept derogatory actions, but accept the person, lovingly.

We are doing the best **we** can too! Our interpretation of another's actions may be incorrect. The outer facade may just contradict the real inner issue and intent. It is difficult to interpret certain things in any other way but wrong when it is in conflict with our definition and image of "right." Be willing to be wrong.

Chapter 19 - Exercise

These questions will give insight into your relationship with a teacher even if that teacher is you.

1. Identify someone you feel is pretentious.
2. List five good traits about this person.
3. Which traits in Question #2 do you possess?
4. What must you do to develop these good traits?

Footnotes

[1] Christian D. Larson. Pathway of Roses. Los Angeles, CA: G&J Publishing Co., (1953) 191.

[2] Ibid, 191.

[3] A Course in Miracles. (Tiburon, CA: Foundation for Inner Peace, 1985) 479.

[4] Ibid, 518.

[5] Ibid, 86.

[6] Ibid, 33.

[7] Ibid, 85.

[8] Ibid, 86.

[9] John 14:12.

[10] A Course in Miracles. (Tiburon, CA: Foundation for Inner Peace, 1985) 192.

[11] Ibid, 366.

Other Books by the Author

- *There's Nothing Going On But Your Thoughts -* **Book 2**

- *There's Nothing Going On But Your Thoughts -* **Workbook**

- *The Obvious Secret Lesson of the Wizard of Oz* – a metaphysical interpretation of "A Course in Miracles"

- Class/retreat information at www.helengordon.com or at www.upfp.org.

www.ingramcontent.com/pod-product-compliance
Lightning Source LLC
Chambersburg PA
CBHW070850050426
42453CB00012B/2126